VICTORIAN

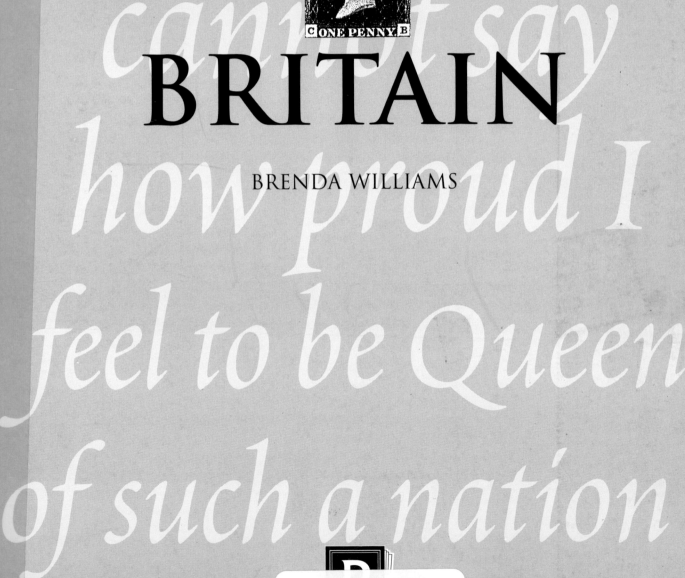

BRITAIN

BRENDA WILLIAMS

'I really cannot say how proud I feel to be Queen of such a nation'

Publication in this form copyright © Jarrold Publishing 2005.
Text copyright © Jarrold Publishing.
The moral right of the author has been asserted.
Series editor Angela Royston.
Designed by Simon Borrough.
Picture research by Jan Kean.

The publishers wish to thank John Cooper, formerly Head of Education at the National Portrait Gallery, for reading the text.

The photographs are reproduced by kind permission of: Barnaby's Picture Library: 11, 63t; Bridgeman Art Library: 5, 6, 9t, 10b, 12, 13t, 16, 17, 19, 20b, 21b, 22b, 23t, 27br, 28b, 29t, 31, 36, 38bl, 52, 53br, 54tl, 55tl, 56, 59b, 61 both, 65tr, 67cl 70tr, 72 all, 73b, 75, 76b, 77 both, 80, 87, 91tl, 92tl; Peter Brimacombe: 34cr, 93tc; Bristol Museums & Art Gallery: 42b; Britain on View: 82; John Burton: 25, 57tl; David Cobb: 46, bc; John Crook: 68; Dickens House: 7l, 47b, 49bl, 58, 59tr; Dover Publications: 53tl; English Heritage Photo Library: 30tr, 69b; Fine Art Photo Library: 63bc; Fotomas Index: 8, 70b; Garden Picture Library: 73t; Getty Images: 13b, 24, 26, 27tl, 45, 60, 74tc; Jarrold Publishing: 35br, 43t, 47t, 51cl, 92br, 94tl; Knebworth House: 35tl; Sampson Lloyd: 4, 50; London Transport Museum: 14, 41br; Mary Evans Picture Library: fc right, ifc, 15cl, 17, 20tr, 22t, 37, 40, 41t, 42tl, 43b, 44bl, 48, 51tr, 57 main, 62, 63bl, 66, 67br, 71, 76tl, 79cl, 81 both, 83b, 86 both, 89b, 90, 91tr, 93cr, 94br; Museum of London: 15b; National Maritime Museum: 89t; National Portrait Gallery: fc left, 79cr, 85t; National Trust for Scotland: 21t; National Trust Photo Library: 18, 29b, 30tl, 32 both, 33b, 34cl; New Lanark Conservation Trust: 49tr; P. A. Photos: 81br; Petworth House: 23c; The Royal Collection © 2005, Her Majesty Queen Elizabeth II: 7r, 9b, 83tl, 84; Royal Library, Windsor Castle 85br; Science & Society Picture Library: 74tl and r; Tate, London: 54b, 55b; Top Foto: 65b; Topham Picturepoint: 38br, 39; V & A Picture Library: 10tr, 33tr, 44tr, 64; Warrior Preservation Trust: 88 both; Warwick Castle: 28c; The Wellcome Trust: 78 both.

The quotes displayed on pages 9, 23, 45, and 88 are from Gillian Avery's *The Echoing Green* and are reproduced with permission of Harper Collins Publishers Ltd. The accounts quoted on page 11 are from Elizabeth Burton's *Early Victorians at Home* and are reproduced with permission of Pearson Longman.

A CIP catalogue for this book is available from the British Library.

Published by:
Jarrold Publishing
Healey House, Dene Road, Andover,
Hampshire, SP10 2AA
www.britguides.com

Set in Minion.
Printed in Singapore.

ISBN 1 84165 153 2   1/05

 Pitkin is an imprint of Jarrold Publishing, Norwich.

CONTENTS

VICTORIA

REGINA · IMPERATRIX

THE VICTORIAN AGE

MEMORIAL TO THE QUEEN-EMPRESS

Erected in 1911, the memorial outside London's Buckingham Palace shows Queen Victoria surrounded by the virtues of Truth, Motherhood and Justice.

THE REIGN OF QUEEN VICTORIA (1837–1901) was the age of Empire, when Britain ruled half the world. The British Army's 'thin red line' defended the Raj in India; a mighty Royal Navy ruled the waves in Britannia's name.

from the British Isles altogether, to lands such as Australia, Canada and America.

Wealth was growing, in spite of stark class differences that shocked compassionate observers into initiating reforms.

Progress seemed visible, year on year, through the achievements of engineers, inventors and empire-builders – those larger-than-life 'great Victorians', headed by Queen Victoria herself.

Dynamic, self-confident, enterprising, idealistic, Britain was gripped by rapid change – although transformation came at a price, paid by those left behind in a 'survival of the fittest' culture. Yet society was evolving, too, with the development of universal

THE WORLD IN TRANSIT

The rich variety of Victorian Britain is caught brilliantly in W.P. Frith's 1862 painting The Railway Station. *The nation was on the move, and the railway became a metaphor for progress – reaching ever farther and faster.*

The British Empire represented much that was truly Victorian: idealism, opportunism, muddle and determination. This was an age of huge excitement, energy and transformation. Great iron steamships, railways, bridges, thundering factory machines – all energized the technological and economic revolutions changing the landscape and fabric of Britain. People were on the move – from the countryside to the city and far away

education, local and national democracy, women's and workers' rights, and a view that everyone, rich and poor, had a stake in the common good. Core values upheld the nation's confidence – values based on Christianity, puritanism and a patriotism that often led to suspicion of 'foreign' ideas and a belief that 'British was best'. Alongside faith in progress, self-help and hard work was a belief that the family was the bedrock of society.

FOUNDATIONS OF EMPIRE

> '*The Aga Khan is held by his followers to be a direct descendant of God. English Dukes take precedence.*'
>
> *The College of Heralds*

TEMPLE OF TRADE

Liverpool's Exchange Building typified the Victorian spirit of commercial confidence, as Britain's trade boomed.

CHOKED BY TRAFFIC AND SMOKE

Gustav Doré's engraving conveys the crowded, hectic, even nightmarish quality of life in mid-Victorian London. Beyond Holborn Viaduct looms the dome of St Paul's.

AS THE FAMILY GAVE society its structure, so the Empire was portrayed as a family of disparate peoples welded together under the benign rule of the mother-country and its Queen-Empress, Victoria. At home, in a nation rapidly becoming urban and industrial, the rising middle classes took their cue from the Queen and her consort Prince Albert in valuing domesticity. Many among the working classes aspired to middle-class ideals; the destitute underclass relied on Christian charity and the compassion of their neighbours and 'betters'.

The Victorian ideal was ordered and God-fearing. Sunday was a day of rest, with all shops and places of entertainment closed. 'Respectable' families prayed in church or chapel, and in many homes toys and non-religious books were shut away, though a Noah's Ark might be allowed.

If Sunday provided moral and spiritual enrichment, it was workdays that brought wealth to the nation and food to the table, whether generated in huge industrial workshops or in cramped, dirty back-street sweatshops. Mining, manufacturing, trade and commerce, steamships, railways, engineering and construction: all thrived on the steam-driven energy and human labour that created a new Britain and a widespread legacy – from landmarks such as the Royal Albert Hall to the sewers beneath our streets.

DOMESTIC COUPLE

Queen Victoria and Prince Albert at Windsor Castle, from a painting by Sir Edwin Landseer. Portraits of informal domesticity contributed to the new popularity of the monarchy and 'family values'.

The Victorians are popularly supposed to have been repressed – covering up table-legs out of absurd prudery, for example. Can these be the same people who packed music halls, sang bawdy songs, read scandalous broadsheets, drank and ate with little restraint, indulged a taste for pornography and had well-reported 'double standards' of sexual morality? They were, of course, like all people of all times, a mixed bunch, although heavily influenced by 'Victorian values'.

THE REIGN BEGINS

PRINCESS VICTORIA, ONLY 18, was woken early in the midsummer dawn on 20 June 1837 to hear from the Archbishop of Canterbury and the Lord Chamberlain that, on the death of her uncle, William IV, she was now Queen. The young ruler was fortunate to have at her side shrewd and kindly Lord Melbourne, first of the ten prime ministers who were to serve during her 63-year reign. 'He has such stores of knowledge, such a wonderful memory; he knows about everything and everybody', she confided to her Journal.

'I really cannot say how proud I feel to be Queen of such a nation …'

Queen Victoria, writing after her coronation

A PREMIER RIDE

The young Queen Victoria rides out with her first prime minister, Lord Melbourne (left), and the reforming Lord John Russell, twice holder of the same office in later years.

Her coronation – an ordeal for a girl who, to most people present, looked hardly older than twelve – was splendidly sunny although not free from mishap. Few peers knew how to put on their robes correctly and clergy lost their place in the service book. The Archbishop squeezed the ring onto the wrong royal finger and tried to give the Queen the orb which she already held. Finally, safely crowned, she emerged from Westminster Abbey to cheering crowds. The 'poor little Queen', as writer and historian Thomas Carlyle called her, watching the gold coach pass by, had begun her reign in style.

A suitable consort now had to be found, and the choice fell on Prince Albert of Saxe-Coburg-Gotha. The Prince arrived at Windsor in 1839, and at this, their second meeting, Victoria was smitten by the young German. Her first glimpse was of a pale young man, somewhat queasy after the journey, at the foot of the torchlit castle steps. Her Journal records the moment: 'It was with some emotion that I beheld Albert – who is beautiful.'

One of the Queen's characteristics was hesitation, followed by swift and imperious decision. Four days later she discussed with Lord Melbourne how she should proceed, and the following day asked Albert to marry her. Their wedding took place on 10 February 1840 in the Chapel Royal of St James's Palace.

The Prince's position was not an easy one to fill. As Prince Consort (a title withheld until 1857) he was never popular, despite his many sterling qualities. A keen horseman, he shot, fenced and danced superbly; he was well travelled and well read, showing intelligent interest in the affairs of his adopted country. He was a man of great integrity but, lacking ease and confidence, never

ROYAL WEDDING DAY

'Looking out of our nursery window, we saw the ships dressed with flags from end to end; we saw the various trade processions pass with bands playing and with banners on two poles ... the Foresters with green scarves and bows; shepherdesses with crooks and ribbons. **The maids ran out to see the fun, and my brother John and I seized on two sticks, to which we tied a woollen scarf, and paraded round the nursery with our banner.'**

Recollection by two-year-old Samuel Scott

in Kingston upon Hull

fitted into the social world of the aristocracy. Albert had the essential Victorian virtues – and a cynical nation perhaps found him just too good to be true. To the Queen's adoring eyes, he was perfect. He taught her the good habits of methodical application and routine. Together they sat and worked on state papers. Together they raised a large family – their first child, Princess Victoria (known as Vicky), was born in November 1840. Without Albert, Victoria was bereft, and his death in 1861 was a devastating blow from which she never fully recovered.

FAMILY IDEALS

VICTORIAN SOCIETY WAS ROOTED in the 'ideal family', whose large, spreading branches granted security and respectability to several generations: grandparents, single daughters, unmarried 'maiden' aunts and bachelor uncles. Members relied on its benevolence to provide most of their needs, from food and shelter to entertainment and education. While this picture may have been true for the middle class, and much of the working class as well, family breakdown and dispersal was all too common among the desperately poor. People moving from the country to work in towns and cities lost touch with relatives and the roots of home. Once in the teeming cities, youngsters from poverty-stricken families, or those with no families at all, fought to stay alive.

Victoria and Albert set the pattern of family life. Their having nine children was not unusual for the times, as more children survived infancy thanks to medical improvements such as antiseptic surgery, introduced by Lister in the 1860s.

TABLE MANNERS
Father carves the Sunday roast. Mealtimes were not always this formal, although 'no speaking' (unless first addressed by an adult) was the rule for children, as was eating everything on the plate.

Papa ruled the typical family roost, from Prince Albert downwards. Commanding obedience and respect, Father's word was law to both family and servants. He sat at the head of the table and supervised his children's table manners. Papa also led prayers for the entire household each day. He took his brood to church on Sundays to sit in the family pew, and perhaps for a walk later in the day. Mama was queen of the home. To Victorians, 'mother' was an idealized figure of womanhood, the epitome of domestic virtue. She kept her many children in order, ran the household and supervised the servants.

Poor families had no servants. For them, life meant constant work to avoid 'going on the parish' to receive the only form of social benefit available. In a poor family, everyone worked as soon as they were able, sometimes from five years old. Much depended on the mother's health, and

HOME FRONT
The boys play mock battles in this painting, while their sister runs an errand and mother reflects on the perils of a soldier's life far from home.

how well she could run her household on a small budget. This might mean the difference between a tolerably happy existence and destitution.

❧

After the 1850s more families joined the middle class, the once-small group of professionals, businessmen, large shopkeepers, bankers and the like who led lives far removed from the working class. But as the century wore on, a large new group emerged – the lower middle class – working mainly in offices or shops, or as skilled artisans. Its members lived in the growing suburbs, in rows of neat terraced or semi-detached houses with small gardens back and front.

❧

The old middle class – doctors, lawyers, clergy and top civil servants – were university educated. Self-made manufacturers and factory owners sent their children off to be educated too, but returning scholars had no wish to work in family factories. Instead they chose careers in commerce – banking, shipping and insurance. But middle-class life – keeping a house with servants and paying for education – could be expensive. It made sense to limit the number of children if possible, and so the large Victorian family gradually shrank.

'Our first duty is towards the people of this country, to maintain their interests and rights; our second duty is to humanity.'

Lord Salisbury, Prime Minister

NEW BIRTH

Women (including, perhaps, a wet-nurse) watch over the cradle as the mother rests. In spite of better health care, childbirth was dangerous for both mothers and babies, and death during childhood was common, despite medical advances.

INDUSTRIAL POWERHOUSE

RAIN, STEAM, AND SPEED
J.M.W. Turner's great painting of 1844 captures the essential magic that so excited the Victorians about their industrial revolution.

'Man is a tool-using animal … without tools, he is nothing, with tools he is all.'

Thomas Carlyle, 1836

FAMILY FORTUNES DEPENDED ON a flourishing economy. Victorian prosperity had its roots in the 18th century, when scientific curiosity had opened the door to agricultural and commercial wealth. This, together with relatively stable social and political conditions, created a climate in which new technological and economic developments could thrive.

Coal and iron, water, wool and cotton were the raw materials that fed the new technology. By the beginning of Queen Victoria's reign in 1837, steam-driven machinery had started to transform industry. Between 1830 and 1870, the output from Britain's coal mines rose steadily, from 17 million tonnes a year to over 120 million tonnes. Coal fuelled the great iron works, where production also rose steeply – from 740,000 tonnes in 1830 to 6,400,000 tonnes in 1870.

Textile industries boomed, too. Exports of cotton and woollen goods (measured by value) rose from around £30 million in 1830 to £120 million in 1870.

Machine-makers were the heroes of a mechanical age. James Nasmyth's steam-hammer of 1842 was 'capable of cracking the top of an egg in a wine glass at one blow, and of shaking the parish at the next'; Joseph Whitworth made a machine that could measure one two-millionth of an inch. Stifling, smoke-wreathed workshops, foundries and mills rang to the clanging of hammers and the tireless roar of machinery. To carry the continuous outpouring of production – and inflow of raw material – a better transport system was needed. The demand was met by the new railways, where, year by year from the pioneering *Rocket* of 1829, faster and more powerful locomotives rattled along the rails.

Ingenuity could bring rich rewards. When Henry Bessemer started a firm in 1856 to exploit his new steel-making process, he made 100 per cent profit every month for 14 years! Industrial workers did not get rich quick like this. Real wages increased slowly – leading Karl Marx, an exile in London, to suppose that the oppressed labouring masses would surely soon rise in revolution. The 19th-century's intense industrial boom was founded on a stable currency, a long period of peace, and banking and business sectors that grew more important to the nation's economy as the century progressed.

There were heroes, too, among labourers and mechanics tending machines, digging tunnels, bridging rivers and laying railway track. One man, now known only by his workmates' nickname of 'Dandy Dick', ran away from home at 16 to be an engineer on the railway. He took with him clean linen, a spare pair of trousers, and a book called the *Mechanic's Calculator* in order 'by beginning at the beginning to follow upon their own road the Smeatons, Stephensons and Brunels'.

STEAMING IRON
SS Great Britain, *Brunel's all-iron steamship, cheered at its launch in 1843 by jubilant crowds as a new era in ship-building began.*

MADE IN SHEFFIELD
The city of Sheffield in 1879, when livestock were still being sent to market in the shadow of the steel mills.

Townward bound

BRITAIN HAD BECOME AN industrial and largely urban nation by the last quarter of the 19th century. Its countryside had steadily shed population as farm workers left the land for better-paid, though still back-breaking, work in towns. By 1901, just 20 per cent of people in England and Wales lived in the country – far fewer than in other European countries. At the time, rural society seemed in economic and moral decline, causing authors such as Thomas Hardy to write in grieving terms of communities vanishing before their eyes. A similar situation in Scotland saw the Lowlands industrializing fast, while Highland crofters struggled to stay on their small plots of land. In Ireland, the potato blights of the 1840s caused terrible hardship, resulting in large-scale emigration to the United States and Britain.

More than 70 towns in Britain had over 50,000 inhabitants. London, now called 'the metropolis', inflated from just over 2 million citizens in 1851 to more than 7 million by the turn of the century if the outer suburbs, linked by bus, tram and train to the centre, are included. Many new townspeople lived in small rooms and houses, ranging from Glasgow's stone tenements to the 'two-up, two-down' terraces of industrial regions and the solid brick villas of the suburbs. Most homes were leased or rented. Owner-occupiers were fairly rare in Victorian Britain, though numbers were growing. Real wages rose (doubling between 1860 and 1914), and the birth rate fell, leaving most families better off by the end of the century. They also had more leisure time. Bank holidays were introduced in 1871, while enlightened employers began to give employees a week's paid holiday.

London at the close of Queen Victoria's reign had radically changed from the city of 1830. It had railways, hansom cabs, cars, omnibuses. The streets at night were gaslit; electric light was brightening homes. There were new and bigger shops:

Swan and Edgar, Peter Robinson, Lilley and Skinner and Harrod's. Trafalgar Square (once commonly known as Porridge Island) had Nelson's towering Column (1840) and the National Gallery. Fast-expanding manufacturing cities exhibited a new, municipal dignity with town halls, libraries and public parks: Manchester, heart of the textile industry, and liberal-thinking; Birmingham, producing everything from nuts and bolts to bicycles; Sheffield, Leeds, Bradford, Glasgow, Nottingham …

Growth was spurred by railway lines that now made their way even to country villages. Henrietta Cresswell saw a branch line arrive at Winchmore Hill, north of London, in 1869. 'The pretty row of cottages where Grandmother lived were pulled down … the holly hedge, dense as a wall, was grubbed up, scarcely anything remained but the tall yew and a golden-knob apple tree which for years after blossomed and fruited on the top of the cutting by Vicarsmoor Bridge,' she wrote in *Memories of a Lost Village*, 1912.

WOMEN'S WORK
Huge numbers of women worked in mills and factories. Here, ranks of women grind pen nibs on belt-driven machines.

ALONG THE LINE
St Pancras Station, seen from the east along the Pentonville Road, London, in 1884. The railway station was a powerful symbol of social mobility and industrial progress.

FRONTIERS OF EMPIRE

IMPERIAL SPLENDOUR

Indian princes arrive in state for the Durbar, or imperial assembly, at Delhi in 1877. Lavish ceremonial smoothed diplomatic encounters on occasions like this.

GOODS 'MADE IN BRITAIN' found their way to every imperial outpost in which soldiers were stationed. Victoria's reign opened with wars in Canada, Afghanistan and China, and hardly a year passed without fighting somewhere. There were defeats among the victories: at Kabul in 1842, Majuba in 1881, Khartoum in 1885. There were near-disasters: the Indian Mutiny of 1857–58, and the South African War, right at the close of the reign. But by and large, the Empire seemed a triumphal procession, unmatched in history.

Even so, the British at home were never entirely sure about 'imperialism'. *Punch* magazine was confused by the very idea:

Imperialism! Hang the word, it buzzes in my noddle,
Like bumble-bees in clover time. The talk on't's mostly twaddle.

The more cynical or realistic empire-builders, such as Cecil Rhodes, might have agreed with a West African Ashanti proverb: 'If power is for sale, sell your mother to buy it: you can always buy her back again.' Idealists, on the other hand, were carried away by visions of sacrifice, heroism and glory. 'A nation without glory is like a man without courage, a woman without virtue,' declared the soldier Sir Garnet Wolseley stoutly. Wolseley was one of four generals (with Gordon, Kitchener and Roberts) who were treated as national heroes.

'… the greatest instrument for good that the world has seen …'

Lord Curzon, Viceroy of India, on the Empire (1894)

Some imperialists saw their God-given mission as bringing civilization and Christianity to peoples in far-off lands. Moreover, Empire brought economic benefits: new markets for free trade; boundless food and raw materials; virgin lands in which migrants could settle to found 'new' Britains. Few at home found much wrong with the whirlwind dynamism pushing wider the frontiers of Empire through colonization. The entire Indian subcontinent was effectively British by 1860. Africa, hitherto largely ignored, was crossed by explorers, traders and missionaries, and by the 1880s was set for European colonial rivalry – the so-called 'scramble for Africa'.

The Empire evolved from a desire to safeguard trade, but eventually overtaxed a home economy faced with growing international competition. Canada, Australia and New Zealand were destinations of choice for migrants, while India and the Far East offered careers of adventure to administrators, soldiers, engineers and educators.

At home, many people simply accepted the British Empire as an accident of history. It did not greatly affect their everyday lives, but provided the occasional flag-waving parade, as at the Diamond Jubilee of 1897, the occasion of the first Imperial Conference. Yet this multi-national spectacle was a last hurrah. Soon, the less-than-glorious Second South African War (1899–1902) signalled the start of the Empire's decline. It would not outlast the new century.

INTO AFRICA

At the age of 24, David Livingstone (foreground) left a Scottish cotton mill to train as a missionary doctor. Until he died in 1873, he travelled through Central Africa, where among his discoveries were the Victoria Falls. 'Lost' to the outside world, Livingstone was 'found' in 1871 by H.M. Stanley.

17

VICTORIANS AT HOME

'The stability of England is the security of the modern world … The English stand for liberty. The conservative, money-making, lord-loving English are yet liberty-loving … They wish neither to be commanded nor to obey but to be kings in their own house.'

The view of Ralph Waldo Emerson, an American visitor in the 1830s

THE LIBRARY AT SPEKE HALL

This distinguished Merseyside property, solidly Victorian, shows the snug comfort of the owner's study.

WHILE BRITAIN PROSPERED as never before, so did increasing numbers of its citizens. A surge in housing supply to new (far higher) house-building standards meant more comfort all round. Mass production, better transport and the Victorian delight in mechanical gadgetry ensured a steady supply of food and domestic products previously unknown. Piped water, gas and – by the end of the period – electricity improved hygiene and nutrition while easing the housemaid's workload.

The result was that middle-class families began to enjoy standards of living higher in many respects than those of 18th-century nobility. Skilled members of the working class benefited too: an artisan's family could live modestly well, as long as the wage-earner kept healthy, sober – and in work.

Domestic comfort relied on many hands making light of heavy housework. Servant-power was essential to a smoothly run household, and all but the very poorest homes had a resident maid to help with domestic chores. Middle-class families might employ four or five people, creating a vast labour force within Britain's homes. Almost two million indoor servants were recorded by the 1891 census. But affluence had been hard won, and often at the expense of those who had no share in the good fortune. Such families were beyond the reach of well-meant 'expert' advice, such as that in Mrs Beeton's *Book of Household Management*. Culinary experience in many homes rarely extended beyond a basic diet.

TWEENIES

Between-stair maids or 'tweenies' pause for a chat. Their daily duties included clearing grates, carrying in fresh coal and whitening the front steps.

HOME SWEET HOME

THE FAMOUS SONG 'Home! Sweet Home!' delighted countless Victorian audiences. In the words of Dr Charles Mackay, poet, journalist and songwriter, it 'has done more than statesmanship or legislation to keep alive in the hearts of the people the virtues that flourish at the fireside, and to recall to its hallowed circle the wanderers who stray from it.'

For families, life centred on the home, where they ate, talked, played, sang, studied, laughed and whiled away evenings before bedtime. Victorians pictured home as a place of safety, comfort and privacy. Yet families with servants had very little privacy. And poor families had hardly any at all: in tiny, cramped cottages, every scrap of space and furniture was shared.

BACK-ALLEY REALITY
Women outside back-to-back houses in the York-shire coal port of Staithes. Families in the poorest homes shared water supply, toilets and backyards with their neighbours.

Parents might sleep in a bedroom with their children, separated by a makeshift screen, while children (sometimes several) often shared a bed, or occupied it one after another on a rota basis.

More spacious, well-to-do homes could be split into three parts: private areas, public rooms and the 'not to be mentioned'. Private family rooms included father's study, the bedrooms, and – in big houses – the dressing rooms of the master and mistress. Guests visited the public areas of the hall, drawing room, dining room or morning room. The kitchen and servants' rooms were rarely seen by the master or mistress; rooms 'not to be mentioned' were the bathroom and toilet.

FAMILY HARMONY
W.D. Sadler's painting of Christmas festivity cheerfully portrays Victorian family values – prosperity, unity and sentimentality.

No ideal home

'In the centre of this street there is a gutter, into which potato parings, the refuse of vegetable and animal matter of all kind, the dirty water from the washing of clothes and of the houses all poured, and there they stagnate and putrefy …

Families live in the cellars and kitchens of these undrained houses, dark and extremely damp.'

Poor Law Commissioners' report on Virginia Row in London's East End, 1838

Victorians loved drapery, bold patterns, rich colours and ornamentation. In a typical middle-class home the best room was the parlour, filled with furniture, ornaments, wax flowers, stuffed birds, dried flowers under domed glass cases, family pictures and potted plants. All had to be kept dusted and polished by the housemaids, ready for any visitors who might call. Furniture was heavily and fussily carved; chairs and sofas thickly upholstered, often in horsehair. Black dominated, with dark, highly polished rosewood or mahogany much admired and sunlight excluded wherever possible, for it faded the deep colours of curtains and heavily patterned wallpaper. No Victorian house of any pretension lacked a piano in the drawing room or parlour.

Slum-dwellers, on the other hand, had little furniture of any sort. Large families crowded into rooms 'with the walls unwhitewashed for years, black with the smoke of foul chimneys, without water, with corded bed-stocks for beds and sacking for bed-clothing, with floors unwashed from year to year, without out-offices,' wrote the reformer Edwin Chadwick in 1842. In Liverpool that same year, 39,000 people were found living in 7,800 cellars. Many were young children, whose home was not a place where 'virtue flourished at the fireside'.

TENEMENT KITCHEN
The kitchen was the heart of most homes. This modest example of 1892 from Buccleuch Street, Glasgow, is preserved in the Tenement House.

THE PINCH OF POVERTY
For many poor children, there was no home sweet home.

*'Mid pleasures and Palaces though we may roam,
Be it ever so humble there's no place like home!'*

Lines from 'Home! Sweet Home!'

21

VICTORIAN CHILDHOOD

DESPITE APPEARANCES, VICTORIANS were concerned about child welfare. They not only developed schools and orphanages, but changed society's view of childhood. Children were no longer seen as small adults, but as innocent, vulnerable, and deserving of protection. From 1842, laws regulated and then banned child labour in factories, mines and chimneys.

One out of six babies died at birth, and though boys born outnumbered girls, more died young. Funerals were common in everyday life – and many were children's. In 1856, Dr Tait, later Archbishop of Canterbury, lost five of his seven children in one month through scarlet fever. Young mourners, often angelic-looking orphans told to look sweet and sad, were hired out to lead a child's funeral procession. Yet life expectation was rising, and the population was getting younger. Thirty-five per cent of Britons were under 15 in 1851.

RAGGED SCHOOL

The 'Ragged Schools', begun in 1844 to teach slum children, were not all as tranquil as this; Charles Dickens condemned them as inhuman. Other poor children might attend a Dame School, run in a local woman's home, or a day school run by tradesmen or a church.

CHINA DOLL

Only the head, hands and sometimes the feet of such dolls were made of china. Once-treasured Victorian playthings are now collectors' pieces.

Many middle- and upper-class children spent most of their time in the nursery with a nanny or nursemaid. Well fed and clothed, with books, toys and games, they generally had to obey strict rules of behaviour, or suffer the consequences – a spanking, bed without supper, or a dose of nasty medicine. Boys and girls usually had their first lessons at home, from their mother, a governess or tutor, or a local clergyman. Unless sickly, boys – and some girls – might later be sent away to school.

Lower down the social scale, childhood was short. Children helped in the house or on the farm and earned a living as soon as possible. Cheaper to hire, children might find employment when parents could not. Around the age of ten, many entered service as maids, gardeners, stable lads or kitchen boys. Others faced a lifetime of manual labour in mines, factories or on farms.

Few children went to school before the 1840s. Even by 1861 only 2.5 million children had elementary schooling; many stayed for under a year and few after the age of ten. Schooling cost at least a penny a week for each child, more than many could afford, until 1891 when primary schools became free for all.

PLAY THE GAME

Team games such as football were encouraged by middle-class schools; village boys also enjoyed fishing and ratting.

TO THE PARK WITH NANNY

A young gentleman, with stick, and his snugly outfitted sister pose with their nanny. The 'pram' or perambulator became popular with Victorian parents, and the three-wheeler is a long-lasting design.

CONTRAST IN CHILDHOODS

'Winifred was dressed in her best black silk frock, with a saucer neck and short puffed sleeves, and her coral neck-lace … [She was] given a rose to hold in her hand and solemnly gazed into the camera for what seemed an unending space of time …'

A middle-class child visits the photographer

'The man in his wild passion laid this (a thick rope clogged with clay) … upon the back of the poor little handle- maker. In spite of the yells and screams and cries for mercy … the blows fell thick and fast. I have seen when the shirt … has had to be sponged with warm water so as to get it out of the bruises.'

Punishment of a boy-worker in a Staffordshire pottery

FEEDING THE TOWNS

COVENT GARDEN DAWN

The country came to town each morning, as wagons rolled in with fruit, vegetables and flowers for London's markets.

THE YARD OR BACK ALLEY, rather than woods and fields, became places for children to play when their family moved to town. Towns were dirty, their streets strewn with 'muck' from horse droppings and air filled with soot from millions of smoky chimneys. In early Victorian Britain, the poor crowded into inner-city homes vacated by wealthier owners who had moved to the leafier edges of towns and cities. Once-small towns and villages, such as Bolton, Preston, Bury, Oldham and Stockport, now had 30,000–90,000 inhabitants each, mostly factory hands.

A survey of 2,800 families in Bristol found that 46 per cent of them each lived in only one room. And Friedrich Engels (co-author with Marx of *The Communist Manifesto*) reported that Birmingham's old quarters held 'many bad districts,

filthy and neglected, full of stagnant pools and heaps of refuse', where workers sometimes kept pigs! In the worst slums, people waded through pools of urine and excrement to reach an outdoor privy. Most poor quarters of all towns lacked sanitation, sewers or drainage; streets and alleyways were narrow, crooked and filthy; courtyards filled with decaying refuse. Factory owners, however, lived outside town, in villas surrounded by gardens.

Farms were growing more food than ever, but as farm workers lost jobs to machinery they swelled the ever-growing movement to towns. In 1871, farms employed a million low-paid workers; only 600,000 were left by 1901. Farmers still hired men at fairs in country towns, picking out labourers they wanted by the signs of their trade: shepherds carried crooks

'An acre in Middlesex is better than a principality in Utopia.'

Thomas Macaulay (1800–59), historian

and carters wore whipcord in their hats. Shepherds not only roamed the fields with their flocks, but also lived with them at lambing time, and it was not unknown for a boy of six to take charge of a flock. Older boys helped with ploughing, and girls worked in the dairy; youngsters scared away birds or picked up stones. Cowmen rose for 4 a.m. milking, while men, women and children employed for seasonal work laboured in the fields from 6 a.m. to 8 p.m., or even later.

Some skills and crafts had changed little since the Middle Ages. Blacksmiths fashioned tools and shod farm horses, wainwrights and wheelwrights made the huge farm wagons, and gangs of harvesters wielded scythes and pitch-forks. Yet by the end of the 19th century, steam-ploughs and tractors had begun to replace horses, and machines threshed and baled the harvest. Trains carried the cattle, sheep, pigs and geese that for centuries had been driven to market along the old drove roads.

Milk came into the cities by train, but without pasteurization or refrigeration was often sour by the time it reached the customer. Thousands of cows grazed in Hyde Park to provide fresh milk for Londoners, and in 1847 there were 40 cows occupying a smelly cowshed in Soho's Golden Square.

RURAL REALISM

In *The Toilers of the Field*, Richard Jeffries paints a bleak picture of the rustic cottage in 1892, idyllic in summer sun, but in winter **'the cold wind drives with terrible force under the door** ... the thatch is saturated, the plants and moss are vividly, rankly green, till all dripping, soaked, over grown with weeds, **the wretched place looks not unlike a dunghill.** The low chimneys, overshadowed with trees, smoke incessantly and fill the room with smother …'

THE ROAD TO COVENTRY

This 1833 watercolour shows a city still dominated by its churches, rather than factory chimneys. The road was to carry only horse-drawn vehicles for just five more decades.

A POOR LIFE

THE POORHOUSE

Ten-year-old Charles Shaw was taken to the workhouse when his father lost his job. **'The very vastness of it chilled us … the sound of keys and locks and bars, and doors banging, froze the blood within us.** … We might have committed some unnameable crime or carried some dreaded infection.'

STREET URCHINS

Destitute street children eye the camera. From 1867, Dr Thomas Barnardo led the movement to found homes for such children.

VISITING THE POOREST HOMES came as a shock, even to so hardened an observer as the journalist Henry Mayhew. On a fact-finding expedition into darkest inner London he entered a hovel with half the roof tiles missing to find three women (one old and two young) sharing a room nearly 3 metres (about 9 feet) square. Jugs had been placed to catch rainwater leaking through the ceiling.

He saw a rag of carpet on the rotting floor, three broken chairs, a table and some crockery. An 18-year-old girl lay on a mattress, having recently given birth to a baby, which had died. The other girl was a street pedlar.

For their room, they paid ninepence a week. The parish allowed them one

SEEING THE SEAMY SIDE

The reforming Lord Shaftesbury hears a first-hand account of slum life. Reformers were motivated both by genuine compassion and a fear of social disorder, the slums being hotbeds of vice, crime and political radicalism.

shilling and two loaves a week, while neighbours helped out with the odd vegetable. So they 'mustn't grumble', the old woman told him; it meant they could stay out of the 'big house' (the workhouse).

The parish workhouse was the fate of the jobless and penniless; there they were given bed and board in return for some form of work. Dr William Brinton described workhouse food in 1861: breakfast and supper was gruel with bread (men had a slightly bigger portion than women); meat was served for dinner three days a week, with cabbage and carrots; on Mondays and Fridays (meatless days), soup was doled out, and cheese eaten for supper; rice pudding appeared on Wednesdays and Saturdays. Although some workhouses were quite well run, most people were terrified at the thought of being sent there.

Renting a small house could cost a quarter of a working man's income. Families on the poverty line eked out a vermin-ridden existence in inner-city slums – in the 'rookeries' of London, the cellar-houses of Liverpool, or the tiny 'room and kitchen' tenement flats in which 70 per cent of Glasgow's families lived. Some slums were newly built, like the 'back-to-back' houses for northern mill workers.

The rural poor fared almost as badly. Farm wages were low and few country cottages were the thatched, flower-bedecked idylls of Victorian paintings. Many were badly built, damp, draughty, and too small for large families (contraception being a matter of luck). As rooms filled up, older children were sometimes 'boarded out' with neighbours, to make space. A farm worker in a tied cottage lived in fear of eviction if he displeased his employer. But at least a country cottager could keep a pig, grow vegetables for the dinner table – and even risk poaching a rabbit or bird from the squire's woods.

'I have seen more magnificence than I ever wish to see … and more wretchedness than I ever supposed could exist.'

C. Edwards Lester,
an American visitor, 1839

LIFE IN SHADOW

Town squalor often resulted from haste and thoughtlessness. Here, workers' homes have been built in the shadow of the gasworks, which filled the air with smuts and fumes.

Upstairs and downstairs

'Be firm, strict, yet kind and thoughtful to your servants …'

Mrs Beeton, Book of Household Management

CONTRASTS IN CLASS LIFESTYLE might produce odd results. 'Ladies look like cooks and housemaids,' commented the American visitor Nathaniel Hawthorne; 'they are not very desirable in their youth and in many instances become perfectly grotesque after middle age … you think of them as composed of sirloins.' Over-eating, a starchy diet and lack of exercise contributed to this somewhat unattractive picture of middle-class Victorian women.

Domestic staff kept fit by running up and down stairs, and working from dawn till after dusk. The maid's day began at 5.30 a.m., cleaning the kitchen floor. After heating the water, she woke the senior staff at 6.30, lit fires, laid the servants' breakfast and took breakfast to the children in the nursery. At 7.30 she carried tea trays to the family and emptied chamber pots; then she had her own breakfast. Prayers at 8.30 a.m. were followed by family breakfast, clearing up and other duties. After lunch, she might rest until teatime (4.30 p.m.), when she was again busy with trays and clearing up. She helped lay the table for dinner, gave a hand in the kitchen and might also serve the family while they ate. Supper in the servants' hall at 9 p.m. was followed by bed.

Servants had a class structure of their own, from the lowest maid-of-all-work up to the butler and cook. In a large house, the numerous servants were under overall supervision of a housekeeper. Cook ran the kitchen, ordering kitchen and scullery maids about. She also supervised food shopping. A butler's public duties were to receive visitors and see the family properly served in the dining room, but his domain was the pantry, where food and drink were stored.

STEADY HANDS AND QUICK FEET

Servants dash to the scullery with dirty plates and dishes. Often, a staircase connected the dining room to the kitchen and scullery below.

TEA BREAK

Off-duty staff could relax with a cup of tea and a cigarette in the servants' hall. Senior staff might seek seclusion in the house-keeper's sitting room.

SERVANTS' LIVERY

Coachmen and footmen often received several sets of livery to wear when on duty.

Housemaids cleaned, while footmen waited at table and helped when extra hands were needed for heavier jobs. In smart households, footmen known as 'tigers' (from their yellow and black striped livery) opened the mistress's carriage, carried her parcels, and shielded her from mud and beggars. Outdoor staff included gardeners and gamekeepers, with grooms and coachmen in the stables.

Jobs in service were desirable. Servants were usually clothed and fed well, and besides, there were few other jobs available for women: London had at least 10,000 female servants looking for a position. Hours were long, but advantages included company and entertainment. An average middle-class household employed a cook, housemaid and maid-of-all-work as essential staff, with others hired for special occasions. Girls entering service, often at 12, started as scullery maids, rising by stages to housemaid, parlourmaid, ladies' maid and maybe even to the giddy heights of cook.

Dinner parties meant extra work for the staff, but also the chance to sample left-overs. After the meal, which might extend to nine or ten courses, ladies withdrew for tea or coffee while the men enjoyed fruit, nuts, port, brandy and cigars. For the upper classes, the 'season' brought a round of social engagements – the theatre, horse racing, cricket, the Henley regatta and balls in London. It ended in August when unmarried men went off to the grouse moor or to Cowes for yachting, while family landowners returned to their broad acres to super-vise the harvest.

THE VICTORIAN KITCHEN

The kitchen was the hub of downstairs activity in a great house. This state-of-the-art kitchen is typical of the late 19th century.

COOL FOOD

Most kitchens had cool storage areas but, before refrigerators, leftovers usually had to be eaten quickly – the servants' perk. This early freezer was supplied with ice collected by footmen in winter and stored in ice-houses.

ISABELLA BEETON'S *Book of Household Management*, a colossal manual, appeared in 1861 after four years of preparation. Offering guidelines on all household matters, her concern was to avoid 'family discontent'. She died four years later, aged 30, after the birth of her fourth son.

'Dining is the privilege of civilization. The rank which people occupy in the grand scale may be measured by their way of taking their meals, as well as by their way of treating women. The nation which knows how to dine has learnt the leading lesson of progress.'

Mrs Beeton, Book of Household Management

Her mission was to show the new middle classes how to give a dinner in the proper manner. She made cooking and eating a touchstone of progress – and she was not alone. Eliza Acton in her book *Modern Cookery for Private Families* declared: 'it cannot be denied that an improved system of practical domestic cookery, and a better knowledge of practical domestic cookery, are still much needed in this country.' Both women were keen to stop 'waste' – by which they did not mean throwing food away, but cooking it so badly that it was not nutritious.

When Mrs Beeton's book appeared, families were already eating meals in

JUST DESSERTS

Mrs Beeton's suggestions for desserts, pictured here, include trifle, jelly and blancmange, as well as tarts and puddings.

and butter pudding, apple dumplings, or suet pudding with currants and treacle.

Dinner in Victorian homes was eaten between 7 and 8 in the evening (compared with 4.30 p.m. in 1800). William Taylor, a footman, recorded in his diary of 1837 that his mistresses (Mrs Prinseps and her daughter) dined on 'two soles, a leg of mutton, a dish of ox [tongues possibly], pullets, potatos, brocolo, rice and rhubarb tart, tabiaca pudding, cheese'. Foreigners were staggered by the lordly English breakfast: cold meat, game pie, fish, sausages, kidneys, eggs, bacon, toast, muffins.

something like 20th-century style: bubble-and-squeak (made with cold beef remains) was recommended, as was stuffed roast shoulder of veal with spinach and potatoes, followed by boiled batter pudding and sweet sauce.

While jelly became the rage after visitors sampled it at the 1851 Great Exhibition (where most found ice cream too cold for their teeth) Mrs Beeton thought it a luxury; her 'plain family dinners' ended with a substantial pudding, such as bread

Boarding-school food, however, as described by Richard Burton, was taxing even to young stomachs. His breakfast consisted of 'very blue milk and water, with a wedge of bread glazed with butter'. Dinner at 1 p.m. began with 'stickjaw' pudding and ended with meat, burnt outside, half raw inside, served with potatoes and 'the hateful carrot'. Supper repeated breakfast, and on Saturday the school cook concocted a pie from 'all the waifs and strays of the week'.

FOLLOWING FASHION

LANGUID LADY
The 19th-century society lady emphasized her slim waist, décolletage and jewelled trimmings.

WILLOWY WALLS
The drawing room in Thomas Carlyle's London house has hand-printed Willow Bough wallpaper by William Morris (1874). The same paper can be seen at Wightwick Manor near Wolverhampton, a property with many other Morris designs.

FASHION AND FURNISHING found a widening market among middle-class customers, who read of changing styles in newspapers and magazines. Mass-produced factory clothing had begun to fill a growing number of shops with cheap garments, while women who owned a new sewing machine might make dresses at home. Seamstresses and sweated-labour home-workers sewed frantically to keep up with changing fashions.

The crinoline, a light sprung-wire cage, freed women from layers of petticoats – as many as five – needed to achieve a skirt of sweeping spread. By the 1870s a bustle was worn alone under a flat-fronted skirt, its complex drapery trimmed with pleats and flounces. From the 1880s, reformers led the move to a simpler, 'healthier' mode of dress, allowing younger women to walk, cycle and play tennis more freely. A more masculine, 'tailor-made' style became popular at the end of the century.

While women commonly adorned themselves with jewellery, feathers, beads, fringes, tassels and lace, there was one occasion to which strict and sombre dress rules applied. This was death. A widow in the 1870s was expected to wear deep mourning (all-black clothing) for a year and a day, followed by second mourning and 'ordinary' mourning, with a final six months during which she could wear grey, white or mauve. Widows, unlike widowers, were not expected to remarry.

❧

Interiors were cluttered if colourful, with glass cases of stuffed birds, potted aspidistras, ornaments, mementoes and photographs, garish ceramics and sentimental paintings. Cheap factory-made furniture was deplored by William Morris and Philip Webb, who made hand-crafted furniture, carpets, tapestries, wallpaper and tiles. When the painter Burne-Jones complained that Morris's chairs were uncomfortable, the designer retorted, 'If you want to be comfortable, go to bed.'

❧

The art critic John Ruskin declared monumental Gothic to be 'the proper architecture for an ideal society'. Great public monuments, such as the Houses of Parliament (Augustus Pugin and Sir Charles Barry), the Albert Hall and Albert Memorial (Sir George Gilbert Scott) and the Victoria and Albert Museum (Henry Young Darracott Scott) represent the pinnacle of this highly decorative style.

❧

Victorian design at its most confident and commanding is found in the High Gothic work of Norman Shaw at Cragside in Northumberland, the medievalist William Burges, and John Crace's state rooms at Longleat and state drawing room at Knebworth. The ultimate symbols of Victorian style involved the Queen, whose taste is seen at her cherished home of Osborne on the Isle of Wight, and in the Royal Mausoleum at Frogmore, Windsor, her final resting place beside Prince Albert.

This ebonized chair was designed by Philip Webb in 1878. Upholstered in original Bird woollen tapestry, it is now on display in the Victoria and Albert Museum, London.

'A gentleman who in after years became a noted Socialist, and Poet, as is an Art Furnisher called at our shop and got the govner to take some orders for some very old fashioned Furniture in the Mideaval Style.'

Henry Prince, cabinet maker, recalling the young William Morris's first moves into furniture-selling

ELECTRIFYING ELEGANCE

Electric light first illuminated British homes in the 1880s. Cragside in Northumberland was the home of industrialist Lord Armstrong, whose library was the first room ever lit by hydroelectricity.

GRAND DESIGNS AND GARDENS

THE VICTORIAN RULING CLASSES reflected their affluent self-confidence in the grandeur of their country houses. While admiring the past, they also wanted the latest technology, and so new mansions often mingled medieval-style turrets with electric light and hot and cold running water. A garden designed to look wild was in fact painstakingly contrived, with plants collected from exotic locations. Victorian grand design meant embellishing exteriors with stucco, decorated chimney pots, ironwork and half timbering.

'Gothic' (medieval). Architects leading the Gothic revival longed to turn simple if elegant Georgian mansions into something vast and medieval. Sir Charles Barry achieved the feat at Highclere Castle in Berkshire, an archetypal stately home rivalling in grandeur Disraeli's Hughenden Manor, and Waddesdon Manor built at vast expense for Baron Rothschild. Modernists also provided their patrons with efficient sanitation and electric light, first installed at Cragside for the millionaire arms manufacturer

SUMMER DAYS

A fashionable group poses for the camera on the lawn. This picture was taken at Waddesdon Manor in the 1880s.

ECHOES OF WESTMINSTER

Highclere Castle, in Berkshire, resembles the House of Commons, also designed by Sir Charles Barry. The great house was remodelled for Henry Herbert, 3rd Earl of Carnarvon, soon after Victoria came to the throne in 1837.

Inside they installed elaborate fireplaces, staircases, cast-iron balustrades, balconies and ornate plasterwork as well as new 'offices': flushing water closets, gas heaters and kitchens with gleaming ranges.

Designers argued over the relative merits of two 'historical' styles of architecture: 'classical' (Greek and Roman) and

William Armstrong. Queen Victoria was happier in the more modest surroundings of Osborne, with its Italianate setting and kitchen gardens, though its rooms were not to everybody's taste. Lord Rosebery, Prime Minister after Gladstone, said he believed its drawing room to be the ugliest in the world – until he saw Balmoral Castle.

GOTHIC FANTASIA
The High Gothic chimney piece of Crace's State Drawing Room at Knebworth, Hertfordshire. Edward Bulwer-Lytton inherited the house in 1843 and transformed it into a neo-Gothic fantasy.

Gardens lived up to the grand houses they enclosed, with terraces, mock-ruins, ponds and large-scale engineering works. Tastes ranged from the oriental (Biddulph in Staffordshire and Sezincote in the Cotswolds) to the romantic mock-medieval at Scotney Castle in Kent, created by W.S. Gilpin, a disciple of 'picturesque-style' landscaping.

This era of the lawn produced the lawnmower – and the garden gnome (the first gnome arrived from Germany in the 1830s). New plants appeared from all over the globe – fuchsias from South America, hydrangeas, chrysanthemums, camellias and aspidistras from Asia, giant water lilies from the Amazon, rhododendrons and azaleas from the Himalayas. Imports including magnolias, bamboos, viburnums, maples and giant sequoias grew as admired features in large gardens. Exotic new species flourished, especially in the mild south-west (as at Heligan in Cornwall). Tree collections began, including Westonbirt Arboretum in Gloucestershire, dating from 1829.

Towards the end of the 19th century, a young architect met a short-sighted middle-aged spinster at a tea party. Edwin Lutyens and Gertrude Jekyll formed an unlikely partnership, but one which viewed the English garden anew, as a place where 'planting ground is painting a landscape for living things'.

VICTORIA BLOOMS

In 1849 Joseph Paxton, gardener at Chatsworth, had a tiny plant given to him by Sir William Hooker, head of Kew Gardens. It was a giant water lily, *Victoria regia*, raised from the first seeds to germinate at Kew. Paxton planted it in a heated tank and later that year, to great excitement, it produced a flower. Annie, Paxton's nine-year-old daughter, had her picture in *The Illustrated London News* standing on one of the plant's metre-wide (3-foot-wide) leaves. Paxton presented the Queen with a leaf and flower.

DEVONSHIRES IN DERBYSHIRE
Two outstanding features at Chatsworth, Derbyshire mansion of the dukes of Devonshire, were introduced by Joseph Paxton: the Emperor Fountain (1844) and, in 1848, a series of conservatories called the Conservative Wall.

VICTORIANS AT WORK

FORTH RAIL BRIDGE
The impressive cantilever crossing over the Firth of Forth at Queensferry was completed in 1890.

GREAT BRITAIN'S INDUSTRIAL REVOLUTION, begun in the 18th century, gathered speed in the 19th as capitalist entrepreneurs spurred the growth of industry and the railways. 'Enterprise', the Victorian keynote, seemed to harmonize not only with business but also with science, where the theories of Charles Darwin (popularized as 'survival of the fittest') suited the nation's commercial and industrial instincts. Victorians were deeply steeped in the values promoted by Samuel Smiles (1812–1904) and his bestseller *Self-Help*, but also in 'social' ideals, promoted by hard work.

FORGING THE FUTURE
Iron and Coal, *a painting of Tyneside by William Bell Scott. Powerful, if idealistic, representations of Victorian industry embodied both moral earnestness and belief in progress.*

Engineers and builders throughout Britain were busy riveting huge iron beams or laying bricks and mortar. Never had there been such an explosion of building and money-making, turning Britain into the 'workshop of the world'.

Shipping crowded the ports; shipyards resounded to the hammer's ringing beat; workshops hummed with machinery; chimneys reeked smoke; furnaces roared with flame. Pens scratched and coins chinked as commercial life flourished in offices and shops, large and small.

'Work', pronounced the writer and historian Thomas Carlyle, 'is the grand cure of all the maladies and miseries that ever beset mankind.' Victorians believed in the virtue of labour, but its rewards were not evenly distributed, and for every winner there were many losers. Millions of men, women and children toiled excessively long hours for low wages, in workplaces that exposed them to health hazards, maiming and sudden, violent death. For its own protection – and usually in the face of fierce opposition – the workforce slowly organized into trade unions.

A LIFE OF LABOUR

UNITY IS STRENGTH

Craft unions enrolled skilled workers, who gave respectability and 'muscle' to the fledgling trade union movement. Banners like this emphasized a union's national importance and the range of its members' skills.

'EVERY SERVANT MUST devote himself exclusively to the service of the company …', declared one set of *Rules and Regulations* for railway workers, in 1872. In Victorian Britain the master provided employment; the servant gave his or her labour. Although a hardworking servant might prosper to become his own master, or the master of others, 'rags to riches' was not a common experience. People who did not or could not work went hungry; there were no state benefits. Options for those who were unemployed were crime, begging or the workhouse.

Victorian workers turned their hands to a multitude of tasks, some physically hard and repetitive, others needing finely co-ordinated skills of hand and eye. The army of workers included city clerks (at first perched on stools copying by hand, later tapping on typewriters), domestic servants, labourers, skilled craftsmen, shopkeepers and shop workers, miners and factory hands.

Factory workers walked into work soon after dawn and left for home up

WASH DAY

Laundresses pause from their labours. Washing clothes by hand or in a copper of boiling water was strenuous, steamy work. Starching and ironing were further treats in store!

STEAM MACHINE
Progressive farmers invested in steam traction to haul heavy loads and drive machinery. Here an owner proudly surveys the ponderous engine he hopes will save labour and horsepower.

to 12 hours later. Pay was as low as the week was long, and until 1871 the only holiday for many workers was 'Wakes Week' when the factory owner reluctantly shut down his machines for cleaning and servicing. But the rigours of the Victorian workplace must be seen in perspective: the vast majority of people in pre-industrial Britain had never known lives that were not poor, squalid, uncomfortable and unhygienic. Workers filing into factories were fleeing lives as farm labourers, often harsher than a wretched existence in the new towns.

In these noisy, smoking temples of industry the machine seemed godlike in its power. Bigger and faster with each passing decade, it produced everything from metal screws to iron ships. British steam engines were exported worldwide; some can still be found working in far-flung reaches of the globe. New mass-production methods did much to 'dehumanize' employers and employees alike, and it was a major achievement of Victorian society to recover some of that lost humanity through high-minded social reforms and mutual assistance.

'We're their slaves as long as we can work, we pile up their fortunes with the sweat of our brows …'

John Barton in the novel Mary Barton *by Mrs Gaskell, 1848*

MAKING TRACKS

'… the contemplative man … is admitted behind the scenes of the poorest neighbourhoods; [he] surveys interminable terraces of back gardens alive with women and children.'

Journalist Blanchard Jerrold in 1872, peering from a railway carriage between Vauxhall and Charing Cross stations

NOT ONLY DID RAILWAYS transform the economy, but also passengers' social habits. Having taken the London to Birmingham train in 1838, an enthusiastic traveller wrote, 'Of six whom the coach contained I knew three. We talked Magnetism and I read III [the third instalment] of *Nicholas Nickleby* … I think railroads will go far towards making us a more social people.'

Steam railways had evolved from horse-drawn railways used to carry coal. The first line opened to the public in 1825, when George Stephenson's engine *Locomotion* puffed along a track linking Stockton and Darlington. *Rocket*, another Stephenson locomotive, won the Rainhill speed trials and a year later, in 1830,

hauled the first regular passenger trains between Liverpool and Manchester. 'Railway mania' gathered momentum as speculators laid track at feverish speed. By 1850, some 11,200 kilometres (7,000 miles) of rail had been laid across the country by gangs of navigators or 'navvies'. The King's Cross to York line opened that year, and in the 1860s the east coast line to Scotland was completed. Small lines were grouped into district systems, forerunners of the later 'big four' regional companies – London, Midland and Scottish; London and North Eastern; Southern; and Great Western.

Train journeys were at first an ordeal. Early carriages (looking much like horse-drawn coaches) were open to the skies,

LORD OF ALL

The Victorians idolized steam locomotives, symbolic of power, energy, work and progress.

and roofs were not made compulsory on third-class carriages until 1846. Seats were wooden boards, there were no toilets, people became travel sick, and long journeys frequently took all day – or more. A traveller in the 1850s described leaving Hull at 6 a.m. on a 'third-classer' bound for Cheltenham and stopping the night in Derby because, although the train had reached there by mid afternoon, it proceeded no further that day.

By 1885, the rail network covered 27,000 kilometres (17,000 miles). 'Railway kings' like George Hudson and Thomas Brassey made fortunes; rather less wealth came the way of railway engineers such as the Stephensons (George and his son Robert) and Isambard Kingdom Brunel. Brunel built the Great Western Railway, with its unique 'broad gauge' track which had rails laid 7 feet (2 metres) apart; Stephenson's narrow gauge, just 4 feet 8½ inches (1.4 metres) wide was the standard distance between wagon wheels.

Grand stations appeared in the cities (London's last major terminus was Marylebone, in 1899). Commuting by rail became a daily reality for many city workers and in 1863 Londoners experienced the capital's first underground line, the smoke-filled 'cut and cover' Metropolitan.

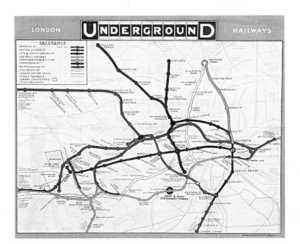

START OF THE TUBE

The 1863 Metropolitan Line was the first underground railway, and the 1890 City and South London the first electric line. By the end of the Victorian era, London's Underground system was running into green field countryside.

TUNNEL OF SMOKE

An underground train passes through Portland Street station, London, on a trial run in 1862. Passengers in open wagons pulled by steam locomotives had a smoky and smutty ride through the tunnels.

BRICKS AND IRON

BESIDES RAILWAYS, VICTORIANS built roads, bridges, docks and lighthouses; they dug tunnels, sewers and drains. They made iron steamships, turbines and torpedoes, bicycles, steam buses and trams. Machinery fascinated almost everyone. Exhibited, polished and improved, it promised fulfilment for the age. Factories and power stations became tabernacles of gleaming oiled metal, humming smoothly.

Building every bridge and tunnel was a drama, and sometimes a tragedy. Brunel's Box Tunnel (1841), on the Great Western railway between Bath and Swindon, for example, cost 100 lives for 3 kilometres (2 miles) of limestone rock and earth. The tunnel was so straight that the 'sun shines through, from one end to the other'. It also descended a gradient of 1 in 100, causing one Member of Parliament to express the fear that if a train's brakes failed, terrified passengers would shoot out of the tunnel at 120 miles per hour (192 kilometres per hour). Another MP declared during a parliamentary debate that, even were the tunnel completed, no one would be brave enough to enter it.

MAN OF IRON
Isambard Kingdom Brunel epitomized Victorian engineering at its most flamboyant.

IN SUSPENSE

Brunel's winning design for the Clifton Suspension Bridge was his fourth attempt. Work began in 1836, the builders being **'a motley collection of hard-drinking Cornish miners, Bristol masons and quarrymen'.** In 1843, work halted when money ran out – a frequent problem for Victorian speculative builders – but restarted in 1857, using discarded chains from Brunel's obsolete Hungerford Bridge in London. But by the time Clifton's stunning bridge was finished, in 1864, Brunel was dead.

CLIFTON SUSPENSION BRIDGE
A lithograph shows Brunel's bridge at the time of its completion in 1864.

HOUSES OF PARLIAMENT

As well as the new Palace of Westminster, additions to the Thames skyline included the Victoria Tower, 1858, and the Clock Tower with its bell 'Big Ben' cast the same year at Whitechapel in London.

Modern Londoners have reason to thank Joseph Bazalgette, the engineer who embanked the Thames to prevent flooding and laid London's brick sewers and water pipes to solve a chronic sanitation problem. But the greatest of all Victorian engineers was Isambard Kingdom Brunel (1806–59), who as a young man had almost drowned in the Thames tunnel dug by his father Marc, inventor of the tunnelling shield. Brunel's ambitious projects included 1,600 kilometres (1,000 miles) of railway, three historic ships (*Great Western, Great Britain* and the gigantic *Great Eastern*), and the Clifton Suspension Bridge across the Avon.

Leading Victorian architects, on the other hand, looked to the Middle Ages for inspiration. Their revival of medieval 'Gothic' style produced its most spectacular result in Westminster's new Houses of Parliament, designed by Pugin and Barry to replace the ancient buildings burnt down in 1834. Also inspired by medieval Gothic were William Burges, restorer of Cardiff Castle, and the church architect William Butterfield, designer of Keble College, Oxford.

One of the 19th-century world's greatest engineering triumphs was the Suez Canal which, though French in concept, was snapped up by Britain when Disraeli bought the company's shares. 'It is settled, you shall have it, Madam,' he assured Queen Victoria, then asked Baron Rothschild to loan the £4 million needed. Rothschild asked what security was offered for the loan. When told 'the British government', the financier replied 'You shall have it.' The 177,646 shares paid for by Rothschild, however, fell short by 40, so the price was amended to £3,976,582.

'The line to Heaven by Christ was made With heavenly truth the Rails are laid …'

From a 19th-century tomb inscription, celebrating the railway

ST PANCRAS STATION

Built 1867–74 by Sir George Gilbert Scott, this was the terminus for the Midland Railway. The vault over the platforms, designed by W.H. Barlow, has a span of over 80 metres (265 feet).

THE GREAT EXHIBITION

THE 1851 GREAT EXHIBITION was intended to show Britain's economic supremacy: to celebrate – through science, trade and industry – the triumph of peace and progress. Prince Albert took a keen interest in its organization. To house the exhibits, Joseph Paxton (1801–65), builder of the Great Conservatory at Chatsworth in Derbyshire, designed a vast structure of glass and iron. No bricks were to be used – almost heresy in Victorian times. It was prefabricated and put together in London's Hyde Park. Doubters scoffed, but the building's 33,000 iron columns and 900,000 square feet (83,610 square metres) of glass were in place in 17 weeks. The writer William Makepeace Thackeray offered it a 'May Day Ode':

> *As though 'twere by a wizard's rod*
> *A blazing arch of lucid glass*
> *Leaps like a fountain from the grass*
> *To meet the sun.*

IMPERIAL SHOW
Exhibits from around the Empire, including this Indian ceremonial elephant in all its finery, proved a great hit with the public.

Opened on 1 May by Queen Victoria (dressed in pink and silver and wearing the Koh-i-Noor diamond), the Exhibition was a mighty success. Fears of shattering glass proved groundless; Paxton's crystal miracle withstood both hailstones and gunfire in St James's Park. Inside, people were dazzled by sight, sound, and novelty. Charles Dickens was thrilled, exclaiming 'There is nothing like it in all fairyland!' Lord Macaulay called the Crystal Palace 'a most gorgeous sight … beyond the dreams of the Arabian romances'. Only the art critic John Ruskin was unimpressed, grumbling that it had 'no more sublimity than a cucumber frame'.

By its closure on 15 October, six million visitors had tramped up and down the aisles (93,000 squeezing in on one day alone), marvelling at the palace and its contents, displayed by 15,000 exhibitors. The *Art Journal's Catalogue* was understandably enthusiastic. 'Forming the centre of the entire building rises the gigantic fountain … whilst at the northern end the eye is relieved by the verdure

PALACE OF VARIETY
Visitors marvelled at the scale of the Crystal Palace, which offered an exhibition space six times bigger than the area of St Paul's Cathedral.

of tropical plants and the lofty and over-shadowing branches of forest trees ... The objects which first attract the eye are the sculptures ... some of them of colossal size and of unrivalled beauty.'

Within this vast space – 563 metres (1,848 feet) long and 124 metres (408 feet) wide – visitors could see working steam engines, farm machinery, weapons, musical instruments, textiles, furniture, and all kinds of exotic products from around the world. They also marvelled at strange new foods, stuffed animals, precious stones and minerals. On cut-price 'shilling days', working families came with their children.

After touring around, people relaxed at the refreshment tables or in the picnic areas, shaded by trees and soothed by fountains splashing over goldfish in pools.

Everyone was impressed: 'There was a freedom about it all, a good humour, a sense of holiday, a novelty ...'. The Queen went almost daily for the first three months. 'I can think of nothing else,' she told her uncle, King Leopold of the Belgians. The profits helped to pay for the South Kensington museums, while various scientific exhibits formed the basis of the Science Museum, established in an iron building in 1857.

TASTEFUL TRIUMPH

'Such efforts have been made,' enthused Queen Victoria, who was delighted with the Exhibition, 'and our people have shown such taste in their manufactures.'

'The variety of colour, the bright sunshine, the throng of people, the sound of their voices, the distant music, the great crystal fountain in the centre ... the trees, plants and creepers which hung from the gallery fronts, silenced us.'

The Reverend Samuel Scott (1838–1923), who visited the Great Exhibition at the age of 13 years

SA
U
co
17
19
fa
G
st

ARTS AND ENTERTAINMENT

THE TATE GALLERY

Sugar tycoon Sir Henry Tate founded the gallery, designed by Sidney Smith and opened in 1897 on London's Millbank, beside the River Thames.

OH! MR PORTER

A popular song sheet features the music hall star Marie Lloyd.

FACTORIES PRODUCED MORE THAN utility goods. Artistic and decorative items could also be made by machine, to adorn every home, however humble. To 21st-century eyes, Victorian art and architecture may appear over-elaborate. Victorians loved sentimentality, romance and nostalgia; they recreated the Middle Ages in glowing colours and detail, while experimenting with modern materials such as cast iron. They were capable of stark realism and whimsy, sometimes at the same time.

The Victorian spirit expressed itself freely and forcefully in many and varied ways: the paintings of Turner and Burne-Jones; the designs of Morris and Beardsley; the novels of Dickens, Trollope, George Eliot, Thackeray and the Brontë sisters; the poetry of Tennyson and Browning. Oscar Wilde and Gerard Manley Hopkins were both Victorians; so were Thomas Hardy, Rudyard Kipling, Edward Lear, Lewis Carroll, Sir Arthur Conan Doyle, Jerome K. Jerome and W.S. Gilbert. It was a rich mixture.

A growing band of readers devoured the latest lengthy novels, the well-to-do flocked to the opera or ballet, and art lovers argued the merits of Pre-Raphaelite and French Impressionist painters. But there were diversions, too, for the less serious-minded. Travelling circuses and fairs toured the country. Almost every town had a music hall. Theatre-goers loved spectacle – pantomimes with real horses, plays with startling special effects, 'hiss and boo' melodramas with leering squires and mistreated maidens. There was seldom a dull moment.

Many performers started young. The actress Ellen Terry made her stage debut aged nine in 1856, in Shakespeare's *The Winter's Tale* – and *The Times* noted her 'vivacious precocity'. She worked from 10 a.m. until midnight for 30 shillings a week, of which her parents allowed her sixpence. Later, after a brief failed marriage, she bore two illegitimate children to the architect Edward Godwin. Defying convention came at a cost, even for a star. Ellen Terry's flagrant 'immorality' meant a breach with family and friends, among them Lewis Carroll, who wrote: 'She had so entirely sacrificed her social position that I had no desire but to drop the acquaintance.'

A VICTORIAN WONDERLAND

John Tenniel's illustration for The Nursery Alice, *published in 1889 for young readers. Lewis Carroll's highly original* Alice's Adventures in Wonderland, *1865, is among the most remarkable achievements of Victorian imagination.*

ARTS AND CRAFTS

RED HOUSE

Walter Crane's painting shows Red House, in what was then the Kentish countryside near Bexleyheath. Designed by Philip Webb for William Morris and his wife, Jane, the poet Dante Gabriel Rossetti called it 'more a poem than a house'.

FOR SOME VICTORIANS, CULTURE was the beacon to guide Britons out of the darkness into which the Industrial Revolution, capitalism and technology had cast them. As the nation became imperial and confident, the art world witnessed a recycling of medieval style, a nostalgia for traditional values that flowered in the work of the Pre-Raphaelite painters and the Arts and Crafts movement.

~

The Arts and Crafts movement, begun in 1888, rejected factory-produced articles in favour of hand-crafted creativity. William Morris was the movement's most energetic apostle. With like-minded associates (Ernest Barnsley, Ernest Gimson, Charles Voysey and Mackay Hugh Baillie Scott),

he was convinced that machine-made manufacturing had sapped the vitality of the native vernacular style. So they went back to basics, and started making their own products. Gimson copied cottage-made rustic furniture for his chairs, while Barnsley set up a craft community in Gloucestershire, at Rodmarton Manor.

~

Although much Victorian furniture now looks ponderous, Philip Webb produced sturdy yet stylish designs. He also designed Red House for William Morris. After Marlborough College ('then a new and very rough school') and Oxford, Morris chose art and architecture for a career, rather than holy orders as his mother intended. In 1859 he married the artists'

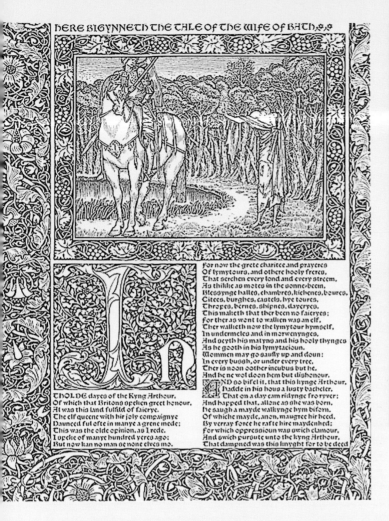

HIGH ART IN PRINT

A page from the Kelmscott Chaucer, showing the 'Tale of the Wife of Bath'. Morris's ideas much influenced later typographic style.

model Jane Burden and, with friends, set up 'the Firm' in 1861 to convert ideas into reality. 'The Firm' included the artists Dante Gabriel Rossetti and Edward Burne-Jones, as well as Morris and Webb. In accordance with Morris's idealistic social principles, the workforce included both experienced craft workers and untrained slum boys, hand-making plain oak tables, cabinets and chairs. Ironically, Morris's products proved too expensive for 'ordinary' customers – who bought factory-made reproductions instead, from manufacturers like Ambrose Heal.

Morris later moved to Kelmscott Manor in Oxfordshire and 'the Firm' became simply Morris & Co. Enormously energetic, his activities ranged from translating Icelandic stories to printing a famous edition of Chaucer at the Kelmscott Press, set up in 1891. He also designed the furniture, wallpapers, dyed textiles and tiles for which he became celebrated. Instrumental in reviving interest in embroidery, silk weaving and tapestry-making, he was also a well-regarded poet. Morris himself commented, 'If a chap can't compose an epic poem while he's weaving tapestry he had better shut up.'

'Culture is the passion for sweetness and light ...'

Matthew Arnold (1822–88)

FLORAL MOTIF

This design is from a folio of wallpaper designs by William Morris.

53

SPLASHES OF COLOUR

TURNER, PERHAPS THE GREATEST English landscape painter, spent his career exploring the revolutionary use of colour. Dominant in the early Victorian scene, he died in 1851 leaving an immense legacy and reputation.

In contrast to his lone efforts, the Pre-Raphaelite Brotherhood, founded in 1848, aimed to revive the purity of early Italian medieval painting (before Raphael). Favouring subjects from the Bible and literature, the group included William Holman Hunt, John Everett Millais and Dante Gabriel Rossetti, painters who grew obsessed with medieval (and classical) legend, naturalism and historical accuracy. Lizzie Siddal, Rossetti's mistress, almost died of pneumonia after hours spent in a bath posing as Ophelia.

Edward Burne-Jones, not a member of the Pre-Raphaelites but influenced by them, was born in Birmingham in 1833. His vision was clear. 'I mean by a picture, a beautiful romantic dream of something that never was, never will be – in a better light than any light that ever shone – in a land that no-one can define or remember, only desire – and the forms divinely beautiful.' Burne-Jones's *The Mirror of Venus* (1877) established his career, earning praise from the influential critic and writer John Ruskin. But Ruskin could also wound, famously attacking James McNeill Whistler's 'cockney impudence' by saying 'he never expected to hear a coxcomb ask 200 guineas for flinging a pot of paint in the public's face'. Although Burne-Jones gave evidence for Ruskin in the ensuing libel action, his sympathies lay with

NAUGHTY NINETIES

Aubrey Beardsley delighted and scandalized people with his 'decadent' illustrations, like this pen-and-ink drawing for Oscar Wilde's Salomé.

'Always alone, I was never unhappy, because I was always drawing …'
        Edward Burne-Jones, on growing up

BURNING OF THE HOUSES OF PARLIAMENT

J.M.W. Turner left his works to the nation in the hope that they would be grouped in one collection for public display – a wish not yet fulfilled.

Whistler – who won the case but was awarded only a farthing in damages. Burne-Jones exhibited only once at the Royal Academy, having little time for its ideas on 'correct style'.

Other Victorian painters, such as Sir Edwin Landseer, Frederick Leighton, Sir Lawrence Alma-Tadema and John Singer Sargent, prospered with elegant portraits, landscapes and romantic historical visions produced for wealthy clients. Although banned as female students from attending art-school life classes, Emily Osborn and Elizabeth Thompson, Lady Butler, were women who breached the art world. A soldier's wife and passionate pacifist, Lady Butler won fame for her military paintings, and Queen Victoria's purchase of *The Roll Call*, a picture of Crimean soldiers, made her reputation. But polite society in the 'Naughty Nineties' was shocked by Aubrey Beardsley, whose sinuous art nouveau-style drawings in *The Yellow Book* and in Oscar Wilde's *Salomé* were considered both risqué and decadent.

THE STAR OF BETHLEHEM

This huge watercolour by Burne-Jones was commissioned for Birmingham City Museum and Art Gallery, where it can still be seen.

THE LADY OF SHALLOT

A Romantic work by J.W. Waterhouse draws on Tennyson's famous poem of the same name. Victorians enjoyed paintings inspired by history and literature.

TIME TO READ

VICTORIANS WERE EAGER READERS, of prose and poetry. The Romantic Movement was still in full swing, expressed in the work of William Wordsworth, Poet Laureate from 1843 until his death in 1850. Next in the position came Alfred, Lord Tennyson, a literary celebrity, as were the poetic couple Robert and Elizabeth Barrett Browning. Yet despite the stature of these and other poets (Christina Rossetti, Matthew Arnold, Thomas Hardy, Gerard Manley Hopkins and A. E. Housman, for example), it was prose that dominated the books the public read.

This was the age of the novel, often published in serial form to grip readers' interest and bound in thick volumes to line library shelves. Weighty 'three-deckers' (three-volume novels) poured from ever-faster, steam-driven printing presses. Their somewhat formulaic plots were satirized by Rudyard Kipling as 'the only certain packet for the islands of the blest' with 'stolen wills for ballast and a crew of missing heirs'.

THE MAKING OF A HERO
Magazine cover featuring the first instalment of Rudyard Kipling's novel Captains Courageous, *1897, written while living in the USA. During this period he also produced* Kim *and* The Jungle Book, *with the enduringly popular Mowgli stories.*

The English novel matured with works by Dickens, Thackeray, Trollope, George Eliot, the Brontë sisters (Charlotte, Emily and Anne) and Mrs Gaskell. While imprinting their genius on familiar social settings and local situations, such writers did not try to emulate (as did some lesser authors of historical fiction) Sir Walter Scott, whose reputation had towered over the early 19th century.

The great tradition continued with novelists such as Thomas Hardy, Robert Louis Stevenson, Rudyard Kipling, Arnold Bennett, H.G. Wells and John Galsworthy. But there were also writers of history, politics and criticism (Macaulay, Carlyle, J.S. Mill and John Ruskin).

Victorians enjoyed the first real detective stories – initially created by Wilkie Collins and then most famously in Arthur Conan Doyle's Sherlock Holmes stories. Cheaper printing had made more books available for children, among them several much-loved 'classics': Anna Sewell's *Black Beauty*, Thomas Hughes's *Tom Brown's Schooldays*, R.M. Ballantyne's *Coral Island*, Charles Kingsley's *The Water Babies,* and, appealing to all ages, Lewis Carroll's *Alice's Adventures in Wonderland* and *Through the Looking-Glass.*

Victorian readers demanded a good story, a range of characters, several plots and a detailed level of realism. They enjoyed time-honoured fictional subjects such as good versus evil, young love, the triumph of virtue, the intrigues of power. To keep up with demand, the output of Victorian writers was often staggering. Dickens wore himself out through over-work; Trollope combined writing a couple of novels a year with a demanding job for the Post Office.

These writers' books still entertain modern readers and supply material for film-makers. But other novelists widely read in their time – George Meredith, George Gissing, Marie Corelli, for example – now languish in public library stores or gather dust in family bookcases.

'Three hours a day will produce as much as a man ought to write.'

Anthony Trollope

THE
ADVENTURES
OF
OLIVER TWIST.
BY
CHARLES DICKENS
ILLUSTRATED
BY
GEORGE CRUIKSHANK

A NEW EDITION.
Revised & Corrected.
To be completed
IN TEN NUMBERS.

GEORGE ELIOT

Mary Ann Evans (George Eliot), painted in 1849. Her eight novels were all set in the Midlands. 'A human life', she wrote in Daniel Deronda, *'should be well rooted in some spot of a native land … where the definiteness of early memories may be inwrought with affection.'*

ILLUSTRATOR'S VISION

George Cruikshank was one of the first and best-known illustrators of Dickens' novels. This is his cover for Oliver Twist, *issued monthly, the book that established Dickens as a social reformer as well as an entertainer.*

57

'Accidents will occur in the best regulated families.'

Mr Micawber, in
David Copperfield

AS CHRONICLER OF THE Victorian age, Charles Dickens was well aware that his world was changing, indeed had already changed. The era of coaching inns he conjures up in *Pickwick Papers* was fast vanishing before that of the railway. In 'The Uncommercial Traveller' he wrote: 'As I left Dulborough [Rochester] in the days when there were no railroads in the land, I left it in a stage-coach. The coach that had carried me away was melodiously called Timpson's Blue-Eyed Maid … the locomotive engine that had brought me back was called severely No. 97.'

Dickens was born in 1812 in Portsmouth but soon moved to Chatham in Kent, where his father, John, was a clerk in the Navy Pay Office. Until the age of ten, young Charles spent a happy time at school, and reading avidly from a heap of old books found in an attic. The idyll crumbled when his amiable but feckless father moved his impoverished family to London in 1822, hoping (like Mr Micawber in *David Copperfield*) that 'something would turn up'. Modest comfort gave way to near squalor. With his father in the Marshalsea prison for debt, the boy found work in a blacking factory near today's Charing Cross Station. Eventually rescued, he resumed school but left at 15, taught himself shorthand and got a job as a Parliamentary reporter.

Queen Victoria's coronation year, 1837, saw *Pickwick Papers* turn Dickens into a success. On the strength of its sales, he married and became a full-time writer. Titles flowed from his pen: *Oliver Twist, Nicholas Nickleby, David Copperfield* and the rest. He wrote 20 novels in all, mostly in serial form, and many other works of fiction and non-fiction. The characters he created are familiar to people who have never read his books: Oliver, Mr Bumble, Fagin, Little Nell, Sidney Carton, Sam Weller, Mr Pickwick, Mr Squeers, Scrooge, Sarah Gamp, Tiny Tim, Peggotty, and so on.

Always an actor, Dickens discovered a twin liking for foreign travel and public readings of his work, which brought tremendous acclaim. His powerful descriptions, characterizations and plots paint a vivid portrait of Victorian life. Not only did he gain enormous celebrity but, by exposing the darker side of society (bad schools, child abuse, street crime, the law, prisons, etc.), did much to foster political and social reform. He separated from his wife, Catherine, in 1858 after apparently falling for a young actress named Ellen Ternan, and spent his last years in the company of his sister-in-law.

Success did nothing to lessen his frantic working pace, caused by a lifelong anxiety about money. While working on *The Mystery of Edwin Drood* in the summer of 1870, he had a stroke and died the next day, leaving in his extraordinarily richly-coloured books what for many people is the definitive version of life in Victorian Britain.

THE MAJOR WORKS OF CHARLES DICKENS (1812–70)

1836–37	*Pickwick Papers*
1837–39	*Oliver Twist, Nicholas Nickleby*
1840–41	*The Old Curiosity Shop, Barnaby Rudge*
1843	*A Christmas Carol*
1843–44	*Martin Chuzzlewit*
1846–48	*Dombey and Son*
1849–50	*David Copperfield*
1852–53	*Bleak House*
1854	*Hard Times*
1855–57	*Little Dorrit*
1859	*A Tale of Two Cities*
1860–61	*Great Expectations*
1864–65	*Our Mutual Friend*

MR PICKWICK IN FULL FLOW
Dickens' first fictional creation has never lost its place in readers' affections. Here Mr Pickwick addresses the circle of his admiring friends.

THE PUBLIC MAN
Dickens was an accomplished public speaker, and so famous that his son recalled walking through London, with 'people of all degrees and classes taking off their hats and greeting him as he passed'.

THE VICTORIAN CHRISTMAS

ROYAL CHILDREN
AROUND THE TREE

ROYAL CHILDREN
AROUND THE TREE

*Bringing evergreen leaves
indoors at midwinter is an
ancient custom, but Prince
Albert introduced into Britain
the idea of bringing in and
decorating a tree.*

THE VICTORIANS CREATED CHRISTMAS celebrations as we now know them, turning a simple religious festival into a great family occasion. By introducing Continental customs, Prince Albert brought warmth and jollity to palace festivities. A decorated fir tree, dressed with candles and toys to amuse the royal children, was soon to become a central feature of middle-class parlours too at Christmas time.

To the Victorians also we owe many familiar Christmas carols. Old songs were collected, new ones written, and all lustily sung in streets or homes by carollers refreshed with a warming glass of hot punch or a mince pie. The mincemeat in the pie would have been just that – minced meat mixed with beef suet, dried and fresh fruits, citrus peel, almonds, sugar, spices and plenty of alcohol – sherry, brandy or port.

After morning church on Christmas Day, families went home to start the festive celebrations. 'Father Christmas' brought children presents, and it was in Victorian times that Father Christmas developed from a sombre figure robed in brown or white into the familiar plump, jolly figure in flowing white beard and red costume. The Christmas bird on the dinner table was goose, not turkey, bought by many poorer families through a 'Goose Club' savings scheme during the year. Often, the bird was taken to the local baker for cooking in his bread oven. Christmas parties meant singing, dancing, playing charades and other 'parlour' games such as snapdragon, in which a dish of raisins was covered with brandy and set alight. Players tried to snatch a raisin from the flames, pop it into their mouth and then make a wish.

Christmas crackers were another Victorian invention, by a London confectioner named Tom Smith. Along with the 'snap', their original contents were a sweetmeat and sentimental verse. More people began to receive Christmas cards, as the efficient new postal service encouraged relatives and friends to send greetings. The cheery robin

A MERRY CHRISTMAS AND A HAPPY NEW YEAR TO YOU

Published at Summerly's Home Treasury Office
12 Old Bond Street

From

DICKENS OF A CHRISTMAS

'When they were all tired of blind-man's buff, there was a great game at snap-dragon, and when fingers enough were burned with that, and all the raisins were gone, they sat down by the huge fire of blazing logs to a substantial supper, and a mighty bowl of wassail, something smaller than an ordinary washhouse copper, in which the hot apples were hissing and bubbling with a rich look ... **"This," said Mr Pickwick ... "this is, indeed, comfort."'**

Charles Dickens, *The Pickwick Papers*

CHRISTMAS GREETINGS
The first commercial Christmas cards were sold in 1843.

HAVING A BALL
Mrs Fezziwig's Ball, from A Christmas Carol. Dickens did much to popularize the idea of Christmas as a time for family reunion and cheerful, good-hearted entertainment.

redbreast featured on many cards was a compliment to the uniformed postmen who delivered the mail in all weathers.

Above all, however, the Victorian spirit of Christmas lives in the books of Charles Dickens, beginning with *A Christmas Carol* (1843), in which the miserly Ebenezer Scrooge discovers that the warmth of a loving family, however poor, can transform lives. Mixing sentiment and the supernatural with melodrama and jollity, Dickens' Christmas stories are nevertheless infused with strong moral purpose, and a passionate sense of social right and wrong.

TIME OFF

'Life would be tolerably agreeable, if it were not for its amusements.'   *Edward Bulwer-Lytton*

CHRISTMAS WAS NOT THE only break from work, for as decades passed by, more people had the experience of 'time off'. Workers were allowed a day's, or even a week's, holiday in summer. Railways offered cheap trips to the seaside, opening up new vistas for many town-dwellers. Leisure time was a novelty for most. Country sports such as hunting and shooting were largely the preserve of the rich, and weekend shooting-parties became a feature of the social calendar, attracting both the aristocracy and the Prince of Wales from favourite London haunts. Horse racing and fishing were favoured, too, by all social classes.

Sport became a national enthusiasm. Ball games first played in an organized fashion at public schools were taken up by the world at large. Cricket, soccer and rugby, developed as team games with national rules, were exported to the Empire. The first cricket Test match, played in and won by Australia, took place in 1877. The Football Association, formed in 1863, staged the first FA Cup Final in 1871. The Football League, for professional clubs, was formed in 1888. Rugby (by tradition begun in 1832 at Rugby School when William Webb Ellis caught a football and ran with it) was formalized as the English Rugby Union in 1871, followed by the other home unions (Scotland 1873, Ireland 1874 and Wales 1881).

Tennis, badminton, golf and hockey were all games either created or reinvented as popular pastimes. Victorians were high-minded about sport; they believed playing

THE GREAT GAME

Football became Britain's most-played team game, popularized by magazines such as the Boy's Own Paper *(first issued in 1879), in which this illustration of England players appeared.*

was better than watching, and playing the game meant more than winning. Women joined the sports craze, playing tennis – despite long skirts – and taking to the roads on bicycles. Canoeing, moutaineering and winter sports attracted hardier outdoor types. Old 'sports' such as bull-running, dogfighting and cockfights were outlawed, while boxing was reformed from bare-knuckled savagery into the 'noble art of self-defence' under the Marquess of Queensberry's rules.

Mainly, however, Victorians enjoyed entertainment at home, in the parlour. Magic lantern shows, songs at the piano, charades, conjuring tricks and parlour games were popular, though card playing was frowned on in 'respectable' households. On days off, young girls working as domestic servants might 'walk out' with young men, strolling in the park, listening to the band, enjoying the fun of the fair or visiting the music hall to applaud, or laugh at, artistes on the gaslit stage.

There was plenty of entertainment on the streets – buskers, conjurors, shadow-plays (the 'Chinese Shades'), fire-eaters, musicians with performing dogs or monkeys. People paid a penny to see a 'happy family exhibition' with unlikely animals (a cat, rat and pigeon, for instance) sharing the same cage. Passers-by might be 'snapped' by a street photographer, or listen to banjo-playing 'Ethiopian serenaders'.

DANCING IN THE STREET

Children dancing to street organ music, about 1890. The city street was still a playground where the young could play without fear of motor traffic.

THE GREAT MAN OF CRICKET

A Vanity Fair cartoon of the famous cricketer W. G. Grace by 'Spy' in 1877. Grace played a unique part in elevating cricket as the national summer game.

ANYONE FOR TENNIS?

Lawn tennis, invented with the unlikely name 'sphairistike,' in 1874, could be played by young men and young women, though long skirts inhibited energetic all-court play.

'It makes the eyes water, and there's a tingling, but it don't burn or make you giddy …'

A Victorian fire-eater, on what it felt like to emit fire and smoke from his nostrils

63

QUEEN VICTORIA HELPED to make the seaside respectably fashionable, resorting to her holiday home, Osborne House on the Isle of Wight, and taking her first sea dip in July 1847. Sea bathing for health had been popular in the 18th century, attracting royalty to Brighton and Weymouth, but by the 1870s seaside resorts were sprouting all around the coasts, fed with summer visitors by the railways. The London to Brighton line opened in 1841, and a new class of visitor began to descend on the once-aristocratic watering place.

A LIVELY NIGHT

'I sniffed my bedroom on arrival, and for a few hours felt a certain grim satisfaction when my forebodings were maintained, but it is possible to have too much Natural History in a bed ... **What is to be thought of people who recommend near relations to an hotel where there are bugs?'**

Beatrix Potter (who did not undress after her first night) visiting Torquay in 1893

In the height of summer, boarding houses and hotels were full – the better-off usually renting a seafront house. Whole families departed for the annual treat, usually by train – although Londoners might board a steamer to Margate. With coastal towns attracting day trippers as well as weekly holidaymakers, the Victorian seaside became an institution. There were bandstands, minstrel shows, street entertainers, donkey rides, Punch and Judy men, shellfish stalls and fortune-tellers. Beaches were crowded, and resorts supplied high-minded diversion (lending

KEEP YOUR HAT ON
Youngsters enjoy a paddle – but keep their heads covered – in this charming photo.

'I do like to be beside the seaside ...' *Late Victorian song by John A. Glover-Kind*

libraries, concerts, lectures, museums) along with pubs, fairs, horse races, music halls and menageries. Many resorts invested in a pier. Blackpool went further, and in 1895 erected its famous tower. In Victorian times, the seaside pier developed from a simple wooden landing stage for boats to an elegantly decorated iron structure with pavilions for entertainment.

Swimming was difficult for women wearing voluminous bathing costumes that became heavy when wet. Lady bathers could be 'dipped' into the water by a female attendant from the privacy of a bathing machine – a hut on wheels drawn into the water by a horse. The charge was usually 6d or a shilling for an experience that was bracing rather than enjoyable. Beach tents for family use undermined both the bathing machine and the practice of separate bathing for men and women. Men had formerly swum naked, but covered up as mixed bathing became more common.

The holiday business took a step further with Thomas Cook, who ran his first rail excursion in 1841 from Leicester to Loughborough for a temperance meeting. In 1851 he took people to London for the Great Exhibition and by 1856 was organizing grand circular tours of Europe. After the Bank Holidays Act of 1871, new public holidays (Easter Monday, Whit Monday, August bank holiday and Boxing Day) became occasions for outings, fairs and music of all kinds.

ENJOYING
THE SEASIDE
A group of fashionable ladies take the air, while the more adventurous take a dip.

WORKERS' PLAYTIME
Northern holidaymakers stroll on the pier at Blackpool to get a sea view of the Tower.

*People of all classes enjoyed the
music halls, with their popular
programmes of song, dance,
frivolity and fun.*

MANY VICTORIANS WERE ACTIVE musicians, singing and playing an instrument. Country bands performed in church, at weddings and harvest suppers, families sang around the piano, brass bands marched through town on any pretext and played to crowds at the seaside. The imperial age produced one late and great composer – Sir Edward Elgar, whose output began in the 1890s – and one still-flourishing musical institution, the promenade concerts, an 1840s innovation reinvented by Sir Henry Wood in 1895.

~

Concerts, the ballet and opera were fashionable for the well-to-do. Music festivals were started – the Leeds festival dates from 1858, when Queen Victoria opened the new town hall. Traditional folk songs and dances could still be found around the country, though they were starting to be forgotten, prompting collectors to record them for posterity.

~

Victorian theatre audiences loved realism and spectacle. Theatre had a risqué reputation, despite the success of actresses such as Helena Faucit (who refused to show her legs on stage, and was deemed modest enough to be invited to Windsor Castle). As late as 1884 puritanical preachers were still insisting that no theatregoer (let alone an actor) could be Christian. Higher standards, and raised pay for performers, resulted largely from the efforts of actor-managers such as Squire Bancroft and his wife Marie Wilton, allied to the public standing of stars like Dame Ellen Terry ('a curious compound of childlike innocence and womanly tenderness') and Sir Henry Irving. These leading lights of London theatre appeared beside Mrs Patrick Campbell and Sir Herbert Beerbohm Tree. Tree acted with his wife Helen Maud Holt at the Haymarket in London. Excelling in 'modern' dramas as well as Shakespeare, his triumphs included Svengali in *Trilby* and Fagin in *Oliver Twist*.

THE JERSEY LILY

Lillie Langtry (Emilie Charlotte Le Breton, 1853–1929), daughter of the Dean of Jersey, escaped convention for the stage. An actress admired on both sides of the Atlantic, her suitors included the Prince of Wales.

Musical theatre was dominated by Gilbert and Sullivan's immensely popular shows at London's Savoy Theatre, and the music hall. Music hall grew from the saloon theatres of the 1830s, although some of its offerings were 'serious' – music from Gounod's *Faust* was first heard in Britain at the Canterbury Arms music hall in Lambeth. Having at first sold liquor, the halls later became 'drier' theatres offering comedians who joked about weddings and funerals, wives, children, seaside holidays, washday and other everyday matters. They also featured singers of sentimental ballads and rousing patriotic songs, together with variety turns. Music halls bred a new kind of popular star in the 1890s – including Dan Leno (who appeared in London pantomime at the Theatre Royal through the 1890s), 'Little Tich' (Harry Relph), Vesta Tilley, Albert Chevalier, Marie Lloyd and George Robey.

Those seeking sophistication chose Oscar Wilde. First successful with *Lady Windermere's Fan* (1892), he was for three years the talk of the town, with hits such as *The Importance of Being Earnest* (1895). Then came disaster, when Wilde brought a libel action against the Marquess of Queensberry that resulted in the playwright's own arrest and trial for homosexual offences. Sentenced to two years in Reading Gaol, he left the country on his release in 1897 and died three years later. He had sadly been true to his own words: 'I can resist anything except temptation.'

'But if patriotic sentiment is wanted, I've patriotic ballads cut and dried …'

Gilbert and Sullivan,
The Mikado

BIGGEST HIT

Gilbert and Sullivan enjoyed a string of comic opera hits, none more popular than The Mikado, *1885.*

BELIEF AND DOUBT

*The University Museum of
Natural History in Oxford, on
which work began in 1855. This
Gothic gallery displays the
gigantic dinosaur skeletons now
seen as evidence for Darwin's
theory of evolution, which was
published four years later.*

THE VICTORIANS LIKED TO present a united
front: the family, the Church, the Queen,
the Empire. And this is how they have
usually been represented – self-confident,
self-righteous, believing in progress, self-
help and the power of money. After all,
Macaulay had declared: 'the history of
our country during the last one hundred
and sixty years is eminently the history
of physical, of moral and of intellectual
improvement' (*History of England*, 1848).
Things could only get better.

Or could they? Doubts and questions
arose in the heart of Victorian Britain.
The Industrial Revolution had brought
'progress' – yet critics argued that it had
also degraded much of the landscape and
reduced millions of people to a state of
mechanistic drudgery, alleviated only
by drink and vice. Religious certainty,
exported with enthusiasm to the corners
of Empire, was challenged by the debate
over biblical truth sparked by Darwin's
theory of evolution. The poet Matthew
Arnold stood on Dover beach, and
wondered darkly what it all meant – or
if it meant anything.

In his novels, Charles Dickens portrayed
a Britain imbued with energy and good
humour, yet often dark and violent.
Reformers wrestled with social problems:
child abuse, public health, universal
education, women's rights, labour
reform, universal suffrage. By the 1890s,
much progress had been made – ironically just as the Victorian belief in
progress was faltering. In such an uncer-
tain world it was tempting to look abroad,
to the glittering vision of the Raj, for
example, for reassurance that the colonies
were developing in the shadow, and
image, of the imperial lion.

DARWIN'S HOUSE

*Down House at Downe, in Kent,
was Charles Darwin's home
from 1842 until his death in
1882 and is now preserved as a
memorial to the great naturalist.*

POLITICS AND RELIGION

THE WHIGS AND TORIES who held political sway at the start of Victoria's reign gradually metamorphosed into Liberals and Conservatives. After the Chartist demand for voting reform in the 1830s and 40s, working-class aspirations took on a moderate political face with the Independent Labour Party, formed in 1883, and the London-based Fabian Society. Party-political organization hardly existed; party leaders generally met at clubs or at their country houses to decide policy. Prime ministers such as Sir Robert Peel, Benjamin Disraeli and W.E. Gladstone rose to power from humbler origins than the aristocratic Lord Salisbury; but nevertheless the Scottish writer Robert Louis Stevenson commented drily: 'Politics is perhaps the only profession for which no preparation is thought necessary.'

Victorian children learned the 'three Rs', but two other Rs dominated many adult minds: reform and religion. Often the two went hand in hand, since Christian conviction inspired many reformers. Equally, the vigour of religious debate owed much to the assumption that Church and State were closely linked. But the 1851 census revealed that only 35 per cent of the English went to church on Sunday, and half of those were 'non-conformists'.

The most significant religious current flowed from the Oxford Movement led by John Keble and John Henry (later Cardinal) Newman, which aimed to steer the Church of England back to its Catholic foundations. Its vivid spirituality inspired artists and writers but had less

THE GREAT MODERNIZER
Sir Robert Peel, pictured here with Queen Victoria, was a principled and efficient political operator. He gave Britain freer trade than ever before and launched the police service, but the Queen disliked him – 'such a cold, odd man'.

ANOTHER BID FOR HOME RULE
Prime Minister William Ewart Gladstone speaking in favour of Irish Home Rule in the House of Commons, April 1886. The 'Irish Question' came to dominate Victorian politics.

impact on the general population. For them, religion often meant little more than respectability and a simple yet sustaining vision of heaven. Few people admitted to being non-believers; one who did, publicly, was Charles Bradlaugh. He and the feminist campaigner Annie Besant first scandalized society by publishing an American pamphlet on birth control, and in 1880 Bradlaugh refused to swear on the Bible when taking the Parliamentary oath as a new MP. He was finally allowed to affirm instead in 1886.

altered voting rights for men by slow degrees, while women 'suffragists' clamoured in vain for the privilege. The same hesitancy undercut attempts to solve the 'Irish problem' by giving Ireland home rule. 'It is the Pope one day, potatoes the next,' groaned Disraeli, as baffled as anyone by the complexities.

By 1901, Britain had evolved a pattern of central and local government that lasted for most of the 20th century. The middle class had wrenched political control

'Everything's got a moral if only you can find it.' Lewis Carroll (1832–98), Alice's Adventures in Wonderland

In politics, Prime Minister Robert Peel introduced the greatest movement towards free trade by repealing the Corn Laws (which had controlled the price of grain) in 1846. His great free-trade successor was the Liberal Gladstone, whose rivalry with his Conservative opponent Disraeli dominated politics from 1867. Progress towards 'votes for all' was slow. The Reform Acts of 1832, 1867 and 1884

from the aristocracy, though by the 1890s working-class power was rising, while the monarch confined herself to a dignified, ceremonial role. Government was now scrutinized by what the *Illustrated London News* liked to call the 'Imperial Parliament'. After all, England was – as John Bright put it in 1865 – 'the mother of Parliaments' and the great Victorian buildings of Westminster reflected this grandeur and confidence.

PEEL'S MEN IN BLUE

The Metropolitan Police Act of 1829, brought in by Sir Robert Peel, gave London its new police force. In blue tailcoats and tall hats, the 'peelers' or 'bobbies' soon became a familiar sight, and by 1839 their patrols extended to any parish up to 24 kilometres (15 miles) from Charing Cross.

EMINENT VICTORIANS

SIR EDWARD ELGAR,
COMPOSER

THOMAS CARLYLE,
HISTORIAN

CARTOON OF
JOHN RUSKIN, CRITIC

JOHN STUART MILL,
PHILOSOPHER

CHARLOTTE BRONTË,
NOVELIST

WILLIAM EWART
GLADSTONE, STATESMAN

WHEN GIVING ADVICE TO a new MP, the Duke of Wellington was typically pithy: 'Don't quote Latin; say what you have to say and then sit down.' Victorians had a strong sense of self-importance, but also a keen sense of the ridiculous – a fact now often overlooked. They admired achievement, many feeling not only that their generation was uniquely blessed but also destined to give a lead to humankind. Had not Michael Faraday, Charles Darwin, Isambard Kingdom Brunel, the Stephensons and Joseph Lister shown the way in science and engineering? And what army on Earth could match the righteous generalship of Gordon or Kitchener, whose stern faces were imprinted on china mugs and biscuit tins?

The Victorians were respectful of eminence; it was, after all, the basis of their social order. And eminence on the whole expected deference. The Queen did not do 'walkabouts', nor did politicians 'glad-hand' crowds at elections. Eminent men viewed the rest of mankind from the seclusion of their carriages, through the gates of their houses, or from the windows of their clubs. They gave lectures, corresponded with other eminent figures, and read one another's learned books.

Few ventured into the dark backstreets to confront social evils – but those who did gained the respect of their own and subsequent generations for their humanity. Prominent among them were Dr Thomas Barnardo, Lord Shaftesbury, Catherine and William Booth of the Salvation Army, Josephine Butler and W.T. Stead.

The Victorian era produced archetypal characters: its most charismatic sportsman was bushy-bearded W.G. Grace, its most famous actors Sir Henry Irving and Dame Ellen Terry, its greatest explorer David Livingstone, and its foremost writer Charles Dickens. Two politicians dominated the later Victorian years: Disraeli, the imperialist dreamer who entranced the

'He speaks to me as if I was a public meeting …' Queen Victoria on Gladstone

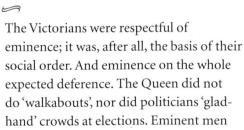

HARDY'S COTTAGE
The writer Thomas Hardy was born in this Dorset cottage in 1840, and here he wrote Far From the Madding Crowd.

Queen with his wit, and Gladstone, the would-be domestic reformer whose earnestness irritated her hugely. The Queen herself, though small in stature, cast an immense shadow over her century. When she died, people really believed it was the end of an era.

Fame did not mean celebrity in the modern sense. Newspapers and magazines reported the doings of the famous, while regaling their readers with details of 'horrible murders'. Photography, one of the great Victorian innovations, reproduced their features. But most eminent Victorians lived largely private lives, free from media intrusion. Gladstone could relax on his estate by cutting down trees; the Prince of Wales could entertain his lady friends at discreet venues. The press kept their distance – though a satirical caricature could be as cruelly revealing as any paparazzi photograph.

IN THE NEWS

'Whenever he met a great man, he grovelled before him, and my-lorded him as only a free-born Briton can do,' wrote Thackeray in his novel *Vanity Fair*. Free-born Britons delighted in reading about their great men, and women, in newspapers and magazines. *The Illustrated London News* (1842) was the first fully illustrated weekly, and the *Daily Mail* (1896) the first of a new breed of mass-market newspapers. While *The Times* 'thundered', *The Daily Telegraph* won new readers by financing explorers, and the *News of the World* reported sensational crimes. Magazines such as *Tit Bits* (1881) and *Country Life* (1897) flourished at different ends of the social spectrum.

FIRST IN HER FIELD
Elizabeth Garrett Anderson (1836–1917) fought for women to have the right to practise medicine and was appointed a physician to the East London Hospital in 1870. Her younger sister Millicent Fawcett was another campaigner for women's rights.

THE ELECTRICITY MAN

Michael Faraday (1791–1867) in his laboratory at the Royal Institution. Faraday's work on electromagnetism laid the foundations for the electrical revolution of the late Victorian and modern era.

VICTORIANS LOVED SOLVING PROBLEMS – and research was not necessarily prompted by profit. Some of the century's most important discoveries, such as Joseph Lister's pioneering of antiseptic surgery and James Clerk Maxwell's work on electromagnetic waves, were made in pursuit of pure scientific knowledge. However, Victorian Britain was a workshop rather than a research laboratory. Michael Faraday, most admired scientist of the early Victorian age, was the largely self-taught son of a blacksmith. His work on electricity was applied to a range of developments, from the electric telegraph in 1837 to wireless telegraphy in 1896, most of them exploited outside Britain.

∽

Not everyone appreciated electric light at first. It was disliked for being too harsh – and less reliable than gaslight. Hatfield House, home of Prime Minister Lord Salisbury, had one of the first electric lighting systems and 'there were evenings when the household had to grope about in semi-darkness … there were others when

TRYING TO CONNECT YOU

An Ericsson table telephone of 1890 and a woman operator at an early telephone exchange. By the end of Victoria's reign, new technologies were transforming communications.

THE NOBLE LORD HERE …

'Visitors were startled by hearing Lord Salisbury's voice resounding oratorically from selected spots within and without the house.'

Lady Gwendolen Cecil commenting on her father's experiments with the new telephone (as he recited nursery rhymes to test the primitive apparatus)

a perilous brilliancy culminated in miniature storms of lightning, ending in complete collapse.' It was not unusual for wood-panelled ceilings to burst into flames as wires became overheated!

Vision sometimes leapt ahead of commercial realities. Brunel's steamship *Great Eastern* never made a profit (being too big and too far ahead of its time). At other times, vision was sadly lacking. The 1865 Red Flag Act – limiting road speeds of a horseless vehicle to 4 miles (6 kilometres) per hour – was meant to control steam carriages, but effectively handed car-design leadership to Germany and France in the 1880s. While British industry powered ahead with bigger, better and brassier steam engines, other countries were left to perfect and market petrol, diesel and electric traction.

Exploration, part of the imperial vision, was also motivated by scientific inquiry. Sir John Franklin died with his men, frozen in Arctic ice, while searching for the Northwest Passage in the 1840s, though their remains were not found until 1859.

In 1840–41 Edward John Eyre crossed Australia from east to west, and in 1860–61 Robert O'Hara Burke and William John Wills made the journey from south to north, dying on the return trip.

Australia had proved disappointingly 'empty'. It was the 'Dark Continent' of Africa that most fascinated geographers, and in particular the source of the River Nile. That most charismatic of Victorian scholar-explorers, Richard Burton, set off to find it with John Hanning Speke in 1857. The expedition partners soon became bitter rivals, but Speke's claim that the Nile rose in the lake he named Victoria was finally accepted.

David Livingstone became the first European to cross Africa (1854–56) and, after disappearing into the unknown, was discovered by Henry Morton Stanley who himself became an explorer, crossing Africa from east to west in the 1870s. No journey of discovery, however, had greater impact on the Victorians than a five-year voyage made in the 1830s by a then unknown naturalist, Charles Darwin.

EXPLORING DOWN UNDER
British explorers Burke and Wills set out to cross the vast Australian continent from south to north.

75

DARWIN AND THE BEAGLE

ON THE ORIGIN OF SPECIES was the book that shook both Victorian science and religion: neither was ever the same again. Published in 1859, Darwin's description of a theory of evolution by 'natural selection' sold out its modest print run in hours. Its author, by then an invalid living a quiet family life in Kent, knew what a storm his ideas would provoke.

Born in 1809, Darwin finished his medical and theological studies at Cambridge before sailing, in 1831, on an epic voyage of scientific adventure as naturalist on HMS *Beagle,* under the command of Captain Robert Fitzroy. The *Beagle* voyage defined Darwin's life. For five years he visited faraway places, marvelling at

EVOLUTIONARY MAN
Before his epic voyage, Charles Darwin (1809–82) had been aware of other evolutionary ideas, including those of his grandfather, Erasmus Darwin, whose work 'I had previously read … without producing any effect on me.'

DARWIN ON DARWINISM

'Man may be excused for feeling some pride at having risen … to the very summit of the organic scale … and the fact of his having thus risen … may give him hope for a still higher destiny in the distant future. But we are not concerned with hopes or fears, only with the truth as far as our reason permits us to discover it.'

From *The Descent of Man,* 1871

THE BEAGLE IN THE STRAITS OF MAGELLAN
Darwin admired the Beagle's *brilliant, if moody, Captain Fitzroy. 'I would sooner go with the Captain with 10 men than with anybody else with 20,' he wrote to his sister Susan. 'He is so prudent and watchful … so resolutely brave when pushed to it.'*

> *'Man with all his noble qualities, still bears in his bodily frame the indelible stamp of his lowly origin.'*
>
> Charles Darwin, The Descent of Man

strange animals, both living and long-dead. South America in particular stirred his curiosity. Why did the remains of extinct giant sloths and armadillos resemble so closely those of their smaller living counterparts? Why were giant tortoises isolated on neighbouring islands slightly different from each other, though clearly of the same species? And how was it that there were 14 types of Galapagos finch – seemingly the same species, yet each with distinctive characteristics?

When Darwin came home, his theory took shape – that variations of a species better adapted than others to their environment would be more likely to survive and breed. Over time, the species would evolve, bearing these favourable characteristics. Darwin did not publish his theory until, in 1858, Alfred Russel Wallace sent him a scientific paper on similar lines.

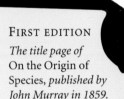

FIRST EDITION
The title page of On the Origin of Species, *published by John Murray in 1859.*

Once published, *On The Origin of Species* was violently attacked for denying the Bible's creation story – and just as energetically defended. The press seized on the notion that humans were descended from apes, not Adam. 'Soapy Sam' Wilberforce, Bishop of Oxford, spoke against Darwinism at the British Association meeting of 1860, but was smartly rebuffed by Thomas Huxley, championing Darwin (who did not attend). During the meeting, undergraduates grew restless and began chanting 'Monkey! Monkey!' as a speaker tried to explain about 'point A, man' and 'point B, monkey'.

Religious uncertainty existed before Darwin, as did evolutionary ideas. But Darwin gave a scientific basis for the 'survival of the fittest' process observed by Tennyson as 'Nature, red in tooth and claw'. Were 'God and Nature then at strife', as the poet wondered? Disraeli the politician had no doubts, declaring cheerfully in 1864, 'Is man an ape or an angel? Now I am on the side of the angels.'

AM I YOUR BROTHER?
Cartoonists made much fun of Darwin's theories, particularly the idea that humans and apes were related.

LIFE AND DEATH

IN 1846, SURGEON ROBERT LISTON performed one of his lightning-fast amputations, taking a leg off in just 28 seconds. Among the students watching was Joseph Lister, later to pioneer the use of antiseptics in surgery. As an experiment, Liston had given his patient ether, a painkiller pioneered in the United States by William Morton. But ether had side effects and was difficult to administer. James Simpson, professor of midwifery at Edinburgh in 1840, tried chloroform as an anaesthetic – and gained Her Majesty's gratitude. Queen Victoria's eighth confinement in 1853 was her most pleasant by far, thanks to 'that blessed chloroform', given to her by Dr John Snow at the invitation of the royal doctor Sir James Clark. A delighted Queen again used chloroform for her ninth and last delivery in 1857, and so encouraged others to follow her example.

Victorian medicine was handicapped by inadequate training. Until 1832 medical schools still bought corpses from body-snatchers. In a verse from Thomas Hood, a ghost laments:

> *The arm that used to take your arm*
> *Is took to Dr Vyse*
> *And both my legs are gone to walk*
> *The hospital at Guy's.*

BREATHE DEEPLY …

G.G. Clover (1825– 82) administers chloroform, one of the first anaesthetics to relieve the pain of surgery, childbirth and – all too common – dental discomfort, too.

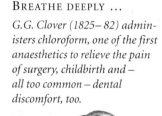

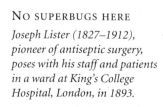

NO SUPERBUGS HERE

Joseph Lister (1827–1912), pioneer of antiseptic surgery, poses with his staff and patients in a ward at King's College Hospital, London, in 1893.

Nurses had no real training, while women had a hard battle to get into medical schools and gain acceptance as doctors. Surgeons in blood-soaked aprons worked without antiseptics or anaesthetics until the middle of the century. Hospitals were so filthy that few patients expected to walk out in one piece.

'No MAN, not even a doctor, ever gives any other definition of what a nurse should be than this – "devoted and obedient". This definition would do just as well for a porter. It might even do for a horse. It would not do for a policeman.'

Florence Nightingale, Notes on Nursing

DEATH ON THE RIVER

An 1858 Punch *cartoon, during one of several cholera epidemics that struck London over two decades. The Thames was so polluted that people covered their noses from what they grimly called 'the Big Stink'.*

THE LADY WITH PERSISTENCE

Florence Nightingale (centre in this painting) was the 'Lady with the Lamp' to soldiers at the Scutari army hospital. She took a team of 38 nurses to the Crimea, and beneath her quiet, gentlewomanly exterior lay an iron determination to make changes.

Death stalked young and old, rich and poor. Cholera outbreaks killed thousands of people – 30,000 in London alone in one epidemic. People believed the disease lurked in rubbish until Dr John Snow traced one outbreak to a polluted water pump. Edwin Chadwick with other public health reformers struggled to improve sanitation and basic hygiene – and slowly things began to improve. Medical officers of health were appointed (Liverpool had the first, in 1847).

Even so, families lived in fear that a child's cough or rash might be the harbinger of death. Many put their faith in patent medicines. Popular cure-alls included Morrison's Universal Pill (good for any ailment; take two at bedtime with lemonade), Parr's Life Pills (cured both constipation and diarrhoea), the laudanum-rich Black Drops, and Holloway's Pill (which made Thomas Holloway a fortune and indirectly funded Royal Holloway College in London).

THE DARKER SIDE

MEAN STREETS

The poorest people of London's East End, like the underclass in other cities, lived in conditions unimaginable in Britain today. At the time of the Jack the Ripper murders, police estimated there were 1,200 prostitutes in Whitechapel alone.

JUST AS DISEASE SPREAD unseen, so the gaslit streets of Victorian cities hid their own dark truths. Crime was commonplace, from pickpocketing (as practised by Fagin's boys in *Oliver Twist*) and house-breaking to violent affray and calculated murder. Vice was easily available, from child prostitution to opium dens. Drunkenness was widespread. In an attempt to tackle prostitution in garrison and dockyard towns, the Contagious Diseases Acts (1864–69) licensed prostitutes, imposing medical examinations. The measures were vigorously opposed by reformers such as Josephine Butler, who argued that they put innocent women's reputations at risk, and the Acts were repealed in 1886.

Reputation meant a great deal to the average Victorian. Double-standards of morality, though not unique to their age, appeared stark when private promiscuities took place behind a curtain of prim public rectitude. Officially, sex was confined to the marital bed, and until 1857 divorce was obtainable only through a Church court and an Act of Parliament. On marriage, a wife's property became that of her husband until the Married Women's Property Act of 1882 at last gave women control of what was their own.

'The policeman's lot is not a happy one.' W.S. Gilbert, Pirates of Penzance

While countrymen waged war on poachers, townspeople bolted doors and windows against urban crime. Sir Robert Peel's police force, instituted in London in 1829, became a model for other forces in counties and towns around the country. Harsh punishments faced wrongdoers: forced labour, flogging, the treadmill, transportation, hanging for a range of crimes – though seldom, in practice, for any crime but murder after 1837 (the last public hanging took place in 1868). These had little effect on simmering backstreet violence or, if fiction is to be believed, on criminal activity behind seemingly respectable household doors.

Murder was the ultimate crime. Its means were many and various – poisoning was a favourite method, and thwarted love, or a tempting legacy, two common motives. Victorians invented the detective story, reflecting their interest in criminal creativity and in the new 'scientific' methods of forensic investigation, as used by the greatest of all fictional sleuths, Sherlock Holmes, who made his first appearance in 1887 in Conan Doyle's story *A Study in Scarlet.* They also relished the gory contrivances of such melodramas as *Sweeney Todd,* the 'Demon Barber' who turned his victims into meat pies.

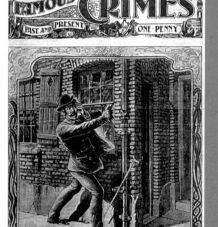

A GRUESOME DISCOVERY

Crime helped sell magazines and newspapers, and dramatic illustrations like this 1888 example chilled and thrilled readers. Here a landlord's assistant, peering through a window, discovers the body of Ripper victim Mary Jane Kelly.

JACK THE RIPPER

The most notorious Victorian murders were bloody slayings in the backstreets of London's Whitechapel. The killing of prostitutes began in August 1888.

'Dear Boss, I keep on hearing the police have caught me but they wont fix me …'.

These chilling words began the first verifiably genuine letter to the police with the 'Ripper' signature, dated 25 September 1888 and published in newspapers on 4 October. The seven known victims all had their throats slashed and were mutilated in a way that showed, experts suggested, the killer might have anatomical knowledge. There was little other evidence, only rumour. Two more murders, in July 1889 and February 1891, sparked renewed fears but the killings then appear to have stopped. The Ripper mystery remains unsolved despite many speculative investigations.

jack the ripper

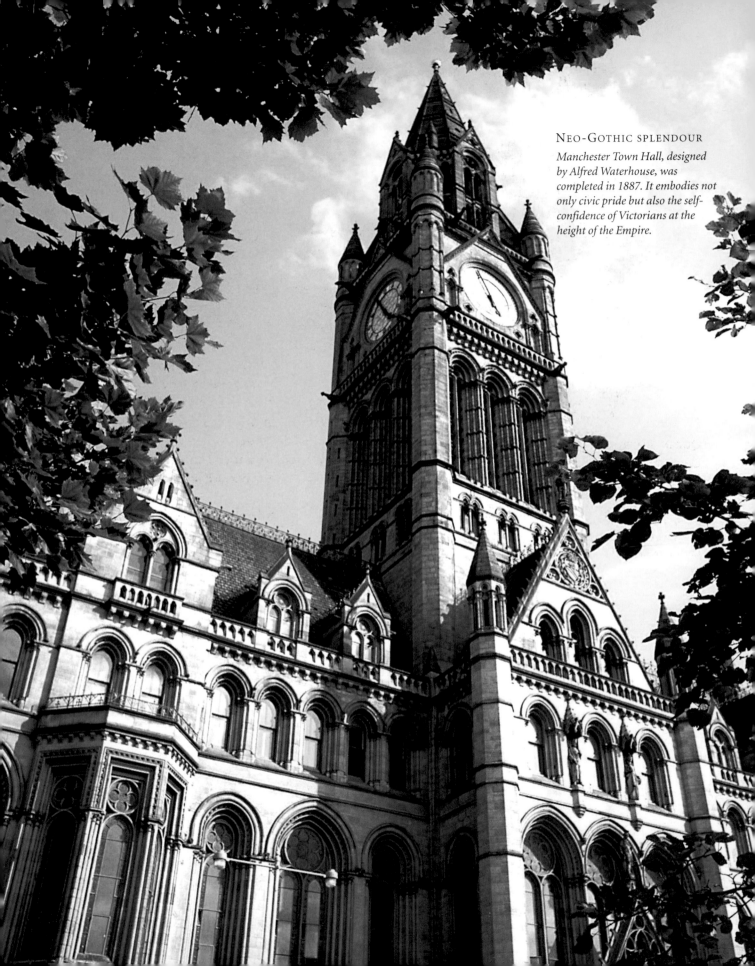

Neo-Gothic splendour

Manchester Town Hall, designed by Alfred Waterhouse, was completed in 1887. It embodies not only civic pride but also the self-confidence of Victorians at the height of the Empire.

BRITANNIA'S RULE

QUEEN-EMPRESS

Queen Victoria in 1890, wearing her small diamond crown and the Garter ribbon and star. Her other decorations are the badges of the Orders of Victoria and Albert, and of the Crown and India.

'COME UPSTAIRS WITH ME … we will look at the maps and you shall show me where these places are.' So said Prime Minister Lord Palmerston in the 1850s, when taking on the additional job of Colonial Secretary because none of his Cabinet colleagues wanted it. Palmerston had wide experience of foreign affairs, but was sceptical about 'Empire'. Britain was acquiring lands in countries far from home, and ruling peoples of whom the nation knew little.

Explorers were meanwhile rapidly filling in blanks on the map, allocating familiar British names to foreign places and opening the way for colonization. The Queen's name had been given to a great lake and a thundering waterfall in Africa, as well as two Australian states (Queensland and Victoria). Albert had an African lake named in his honour, too, and a Canadian province (Alberta). The world's highest mountain (not an official imperial possession but as good as) was named in 1863 after the Surveyor-General of India, Sir George Everest.

Briefly, in the second half of Victoria's reign, the Empire was everything; imperial images adorned tea caddies, sauce bottles and cheap plaster ornaments. Schoolchildren paraded on Empire Day, vast areas of the world map were printed in pink, and imperial soldiers such as 'Chinese' Gordon and Kitchener of Khartoum became household names. When the art critic Ruskin inquired plaintively, 'Who is the Sudan?' he was sadly out of touch: most schoolchildren could have told him. On 24 May each year, across the Empire, soldiers and civilians raised their glasses to toast the Queen's birthday: 'The Queen – God Bless Her!'

CHAMPAGNE AND BEER ALL ROUND
Golden Jubilee humour of 1887 shows the Lion and the Unicorn banqueting with Queen Victoria.

THE ROYAL FAMILY

This 1844 watercolour by Joseph Nash shows Queen Victoria and King Louis Philippe of France setting out for a drive from Windsor Castle, in a charabanc he had presented to her.

ON HEARING AT THE age of eleven how near to the throne she stood, Princess Victoria vowed 'I will be good'. And throughout her long reign of 63 years, even at her most trying, this remained her aim. Part of Queen Victoria's claim to greatness

rests on her rescue of the Royal Family from the disrepute into which it had sunk. The family lives of her uncles, particularly George IV, had aroused public ridicule. In contrast, Victoria and Albert showed by example the value of

diligence, hard work and a happy family life – the 'Victorian values' now regarded with some nostalgia.

Always robust and energetic, the Queen enjoyed good health throughout her life, though the shattering blow of Albert's early death in 1861 sent her into seclusion for years. Her large family gave much joy, but also considerable anxiety – particularly 'Bertie', Prince of Wales and the future King Edward VII, whose character and conduct seemed to the Queen to fall short of her ideal (the conscientious and moral Albert). At her death in 1901 Victoria was related directly, or by her children's marriages, to the royal houses of Germany, Russia, Greece, Romania, Sweden, Denmark, Norway and Belgium. The Tsar of All the Russias was her 'dear Nicky'; Kaiser Wilhelm II of Germany was her grandson, 'Willy'.

The Queen and Prince Albert improved Buckingham Palace, their main London residence, but found its grand rooms ill-suited for a young family. Their search for privacy took them to Osborne on the Isle of Wight, a modest house and estate which they bought in 1845 for £26,000. It became their 'dear little home' and favourite summer holiday resort.

The Royal Family also sought a life of their own in Scotland, at Balmoral, and at Sandringham in Norfolk. Windsor Castle, Victoria and Albert's honeymoon choice, became the scene of family Christmases – enlivened by the Prince's innovations such as the Christmas tree. But Windsor was later to be the scene of family tragedy when Albert, never as physically resilient as his wife, succumbed to chill and fever. Despite all medical efforts, he died on 14 December 1861.

It took the Queen ten years to resume normal life after Albert's death. Although striving to keep up with the stream of state business, her neurotic behaviour caused concern, and government ministers frequently found her difficult. Eventually, sustained by her favourite servants, correspondence with her married children, and pride in the Empire and its armed forces, she recovered her spirit. Her jubilees of 1887 and 1897 were triumphant celebrations, and she was moved by the public affection of the huge crowds.

The Queen particularly missed her daughters, as they married and moved elsewhere. On the day her youngest daughter, Princess Beatrice, married Prince Henry of Battenberg in 1885, she wrote: 'I bore up bravely till the departure and then fairly gave way. I remained quietly upstairs and when I heard the cheering and "God save the Queen", I stopped my ears and cried bitterly.'

'Children though often a source of anxiety and difficulty are a great blessing, and cheer and brighten up life.'

Queen Victoria

PET PICTURE

Both Queen Victoria and Prince Albert made many etchings of their favourite pets. This one by the Queen is initialled and dated 1840 – the year of her marriage.

THE THIN RED LINE

SOLDIERS OF THE QUEEN

Queen Victoria inspects guardsmen who have returned wounded from the Crimea, at Buckingham Palace in 1855. The first Victoria Crosses, awarded to 62 officers and soldiers, were presented by the Queen in 1857.

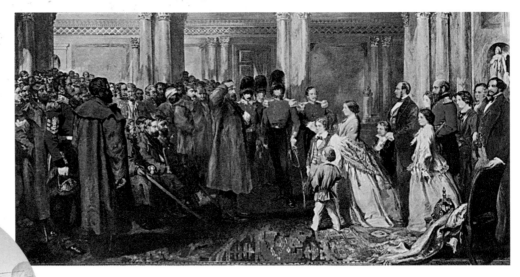

LAST ZULU BATTLE

The fighting qualities of Zulu regiments, or impis, won the respect of the British. But the Zulus finally succumbed to superior fire-power at Ulundi, in 1879, the last battle of the Zulu War.

'OH, IT'S TOMMY THIS, an' Tommy that, an' Chuck him out, the brute! But it's "Saviour of 'is country" when the guns begin to shoot', observed Rudyard Kipling, well aware that the British Army abroad was always more popular than the British Army at home.

The Army that still dwelt on the fading glories of Waterloo (1815) was called on to fight only one major European war – in the Crimea (1854–56), when Britain and France joined forces to defend Turkey, the 'sick man of Europe' from the predations of the 'Russian bear'. It was not a glorious campaign. Press reports revealed shocking numbers of men dying from neglected wounds, dirt and disease – despite the heroism of Florence Nightingale's nurses, and others such as Mary Seacole, a volunteer from Jamaica, who travelled at her own expense to the Crimea. The Queen identified herself with the gallantry and suffering of her troops as if 'they were my own children'. Their stoical endurance aroused the public's admiration as they

read war despatches in newspapers and, for the first time, saw photographs taken on the battlefield.

In its imperial campaigns, the Army usually had the advantage in fire-power, as weapons became more deadly. Breech-loading mechanisms increased the rate at which rifles and field guns could fire. In 1898, at the Battle of Omdurman in the Sudan, these weapons and Maxim machine guns killed 27,000 Dervishes, while British casualties numbered 350. That battle included the Army's last great cavalry charge, experienced and recorded by a young Winston Churchill, riding with the 21st Lancers. Although a gallant action, such charges by horsemen were now out of date. Swords and lances were no match for spitting machine guns.

By the end of Victoria's reign, soldiers had abandoned redcoats for khaki, though the 'thin red line' was still on the frontier – sweating, marching and grumbling. The Indian Army was the Empire's largest fighting force. Successful generals were national heroes, and the public avidly read of gallant actions such as the defence of Rorke's Drift in 1879, when 140 soldiers beat off an attack by some 3,000 South African Zulus.

~

The South African War (1899–1902) against independence-seeking, Dutch-speaking Boers attracted more jingoism, but less glory. Winston Churchill reported this last Victorian war for the *Morning Post*, Conan Doyle ran a field hospital, Gandhi carried stretchers, and the intrepid traveller Mary Kingsley died of fever nursing wounded soldiers. Queen Victoria sent each one of her soldiers a tin of chocolate with New Year good wishes, but the sharpshooting Boers proved dogged opponents. British short-comings in leadership, equipment and tactics were painfully revealed.

THE ALMA

Victory at the Alma River in September 1854 encouraged Britain and France to hope for a swift decision in the Crimea. But with the Russian retreat to Sevastopol, stalemate ensued.

BROKEN SWORDS AT SUAKIM

'After our troops had driven the Dervishes from the trenches before Suakim, the Hussars charged. **Captain Graham, riding at the head of his men, spitted a horseman as one would a piece of bread on a toasting fork. At the first onset, several of our sabres broke over the enemy spears.'**

Report of an incident during the Army's campaign in the Sudan, 1889

'Gathering speed at every stride they flew towards that thin red streak tipped with steel.'

War correspondent Sir William Russell in the Crimea, 1854, watching the 93rd Highlanders resisting Russian cavalry

THE ROYAL NAVY

GUN DRILL

Barefoot gunners prepare to fire an Armstrong breech-loader, an early rifled gun, tried – unsuccessfully – on HMS Warrior *in 1860. Twelve men were needed to load, aim and fire two such guns: one to port, one to starboard. The illustration is by J.E. Wigston.*

IN 1845, THE ADMIRALTY held a tug-of-war to test the relative merits of paddle wheels and screw propellers. The contestants in this stern-to-stern contest were the screw-propelled *Rattler* and the paddle-driven *Alecto*. *Rattler* won decisively, proving the superiority of the screw propeller. Yet the Royal Navy was still taking delivery of wooden sailing ships into the 1860s. Admirals were reluctant to forsake sails for steam, on the grounds that a sailing ship could stay at sea anywhere for an unlimited period, whereas steamships had to rely on 'coaling' stations around the world. Nor did Admirals want to give up the broadside (guns ranged along the decks) for new turret guns that could fire in all directions without the ship changing course. But in the end, the turreted, mastless ship became the naval norm – HMS *Devastation* (1871) being armed with four 12-inch muzzle-loading guns in twin turrets.

British policy after 1880 was to have a fleet at least twice the size of any European rival. To quell an insurgency, the Fleet had only to show on the horizon, flags fluttering and big guns trained on the nearest rebel stronghold. International crises were often settled by the merest hint of naval action; Britain's shortest war was fought by the Navy in 1896, when a 38-minute bombardment of Zanzibar, off the coast of East Africa, intimidated the local sultan into surrendering. His grateful successor awarded the Brilliant Star of Zanzibar to Rear-Admiral Harry Holdsworth Rawson, the British commander.

SAILOR STITCH-UP

Schoolboys aiming to be officers joined the Navy as midshipmen. They needed stout hearts and strong limbs to play 'follow-my-leader' up and down the rigging in heavy seas – and the captain seemed to have eyes in the back of his head. One lad, caught with his hands in his pockets, stood quaking as the captain summoned the sailmaker's mate. **'Sew this young gentleman's hands up in his pockets,'** he ordered. As the first stitch went in, the captain relented, **'but if I see your hands there again, there they'll be for a week.'**

'As they passed the warships Invincible and Inflexible, *the crews cheered ... giving groans for Arabi Pasha, whom the sailors had christened "Horrible Pasha".*'

From an 1882 magazine reporting a 'gunboat action' in Egypt against the nationalist leader Arabi Pasha

Seafaring remained physically demanding. Few industrial workers had tougher jobs than a Navy stoker, shovelling coal deep inside a sweltering boiler-room. But pay and conditions improved, as did officer training in the naval colleges, while discipline grew more humane – there was no more flogging after 1879. The Victorian 'tar' became a national symbol of good-natured heroism, and a boost in public respect for the Navy resulted from the sterling work of naval brigades (often shore parties manning naval guns) in numerous colonial wars. The 'senior service' was riding high, and the Jubilee reviews of the 1880s and 1890s showed the Grand Fleet at its most splendid.

FLEET REVIEW

In 1897 the Queen inspected a mighty line of her warships at the Spithead Review. Victoria had seen wooden battleships evolve into steam-powered iron-clads during her reign.

ROAR TO THE FUTURE

The speed of Parsons' steam-turbine Turbinia astonished onlookers at the 1897 Jubilee naval review. This small craft was the first turbine ship.

END OF A LIFE AND AN ERA

Royal mourners, led by King Edward VII with Kaiser Wilhelm of Germany, follow the Queen's coffin at her funeral in 1901.

MUCH AMUSED

This photo of the Queen laughing was captured during her Golden Jubilee in 1887.

CELEBRATING HER REIGN

Crowds waiting in brilliant sunshine outside the National Gallery in Trafalgar Square as the Queen drives to her Diamond Jubilee service, 22 June 1897. A film shot of the procession seemed to the Queen 'very wonderful, if a little hazy.'

'NO-ONE EVER, I believe, met with such an ovation as was given to me, passing through those six miles of streets.' So wrote Queen Victoria of her Diamond Jubilee procession. From 1876, when she was proclaimed Empress of India, the tide of majesty had rolled on serenely. The Queen headed an empire that seemed to grow greater with each passing year.

Sharing public enthusiasm for the Empire, the Queen was particularly sympathetic to the men of the armed forces. Along with her subjects, she followed closely events in the Egyptian sands, South African veldt or Afghan mountains, and was jealous of her right to communicate directly with her generals: 'The Queen always *has* telegraphed direct to her Generals, and always will do so, as they *value* that and *don't* care near so much for a mere official message.'

In Queen Victoria, this hugely diverse age found its true symbol. Her Jubilees felt almost like a deification for the diminutive 'Mother of the Empire'. Molly Thomas described the 1887 celebrations in the streets of London: 'Almost every shop had some sign lighted up with lamps or gas … men and women in little groups were dancing to the music of concertinas and gangs of youths were making nuisances of themselves by parading in long caterpillars … through the throng. There was no traffic in Oxford Street, which was just as well, for it could not have moved.'

The Queen lived to enjoy her Diamond Jubilee ten years later, by which time the century, her life, reign, and the age to which she gave her name were close to their end. She died at Osborne House on 22 January 1901, surrounded by children and grandchildren.

VICTORIAN LEGACY

THE MODERN WORLD BEGAN with the Victorians. Their Herculean endeavours allied the new power of the machine with the strength and determination of men and women. They reached peaks of brilliant, practical originality in technology and art. They moulded society with attitudes and beliefs that survived the passing of the Queen who gave her name to the age.

MUNICIPAL PRIDE

Birmingham's fine council chamber and art gallery date from 1881. Work on these city buildings began while Joseph Chamberlain, a famous son of the city, was mayor.

ARTS WITH SCIENCE

The Albert Memorial in Kensington Gardens was designed by Sir George Gilbert Scott and erected 1863–76. Prince Albert sits holding the catalogue of the 1851 Great Exhibition, with 178 notables from the arts and sciences carved around him. Opposite the memorial, the Royal Albert Hall, 1867–71, was designed by Francis Fowke. A frieze around its dome illustrates 'The Triumphs of Art and Science' – a very Victorian concept.

The explosive energy of the Victorians spread out from the British Isles, rippling to every part of the globe. Centuries of social, economic, religious and political evolution led up to a rare moment (for it was no more than a moment in the long perspective of history) of vibrant, confident expression. In changing Britain, it also shaped the development of other nations – both big (India, Canada, Australia, New Zealand, South Africa) and small, from the islands of the Caribbean to the atolls of the Pacific Ocean.

But the effervescence of the Diamond Jubilee could not last. Within 20 years the bubbles had burst, and the trench slaughter of the First World War cast a grim shadow. Within 70 years, the Empire on which the sun never set had all but vanished into history. It was replaced by a Commonwealth whose members – though no longer bound to the 'mother country' – still maintain ties with the Crown and share common interests, from cricket to commerce and cultural exchange. Migration from Britain helped to create some Commonwealth countries, while 20th-century immigration, mostly from the Commonwealth, created a new, more diverse Britain.

The Victorian legacy has been much analysed. Their art and architecture, once derided as fussy and derivative, now excite interest and admiration, with paintings and sculpture commanding high saleroom prices. Their novels are recognized as among the greatest in the English language and their best poets and prose writers remain among the foremost of any nation, though some authors once highly regarded are now little read outside academic circles. Photographs preserve a priceless record of Victorian life, from

VICTORIAN EXOTICA
Victorian love of exotic plants led to the construction of gigantic glasshouses to nurture them, such as the Temperate House at the Royal Botanical Gardens, Kew.

farms to factories, with images from all classes of society. A few scratchy sound recordings and flickering films give tantalising glimpses of the people themselves: we can actually hear Tennyson's Lincolnshire accent, and catch echoes of the music hall from performers such as Marie Lloyd.

Many of the world's most popular pastimes and team games began in Victorian schools, university clubs, family gardens and country houses. To the Victorians, too, we owe modern newspapers and magazines, poster advertising, package holidays and tourism, winter sports, the seaside, charity work, trade

ALBERT'S MUSEUM
London's Victoria and Albert Museum grew out of the 1852 'Museum of Manufactures'. Prince Albert had much to do with its establishment, though the present buildings date from 1899–1909. Queen Victoria laid the foundation stone for this new museum in Kensington, and requested the new name.

CARPET FACTORY
RUNS RIOT

The Templeton Business Centre in Glasgow was built in 1889 as a carpet factory. This stylish building was modelled on the Doge's Palace in Venice.

unions, lifeboats, the police force, nursing training, children's homes, the National Trust, national museums, military pageantry, even the English cooked breakfast. The list is practically endless!

Despite the barriers of class, wealth and education, people did rise from humble beginnings, though most 'self-made' men then tried to join the landed gentry. William Robertson enlisted as an army private in 1877, and rose to become a field marshal. The very poor were prepared to scrimp to pay for their children's schooling, and the chance to 'better themselves'.

As the mood of Victorian Britain grew more self-satisfied and complacent, innovation was less evident. With all their capital and engineering skill, Victorian Britons might well have invented the fountain pen, electric lift, typewriter, car and aeroplane – but did not. Nor did a society with plenty of domestic staff see the need to invest in labour-saving gadgets. Such novelties as the safety pin, zip fastener and cornflakes were left to the Americans, who with the Germans had by 1900 become Britain's major commercial rivals.

Nevertheless, the Victorians gave us much that we take for granted: the railway network (now much reduced) and roads, reshaped towns and cities, a reorganized countryside. They introduced factory production, home plumbing, cookery books, sewing machines, family photos, street lighting and public libraries. They made the best ships in the world. They invented postage stamps, cardigans, wellington boots, bowler hats and garden makeovers. They also took up overseas inventions with enthusiasm. Victorians were the first Britons to strike a safety match, open a tin of food, build with Portland cement, manufacture steel in a blast furnace, make telephone calls, switch on electric light, and watch moving pictures on screen – all of them significant advances.

The Victorians left us our local government structure, the sewers beneath our streets, and many of our municipal buildings and churches. Bridges designed for their steam trains and horse wagons carry our inter-city expresses, cars and lorries. Statues of the great Victorians who engineered a changed world now stand in our parks and squares. Although some names on the plinths are no longer well known, the figures above them bear poses and expressions often richly evocative of the age in which they were erected. The Victorians knew what or whom they wanted on plinths in Trafalgar Square; Britons in the 21st century are less sure of who or what to look up to.

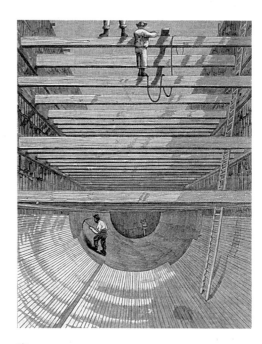

UNSEEN LEGACY

City drainage and sewer systems owe much to the energy of Victorian engineers, and the muscles of Victorian workmen.

INDEX